150 YEARS

OF

COOL LAW

BY

MERLE F. WILBERDING

PUBLISHED BY

HIGH VIEW LIBRARY
DAYTON, OHIO
2003

150 YEARS OF COOL LAW

Library of Congress Control Number: 2002109794

ISBN 0-9667588-1-1

First Edition

5 4 3 2 1

HIGH VIEW LIBRARY

33 West First Street, Suite 600
Dayton, Ohio 45402
937-449-5772
E-Mail: wilberding@coollaw.com

Printed in the United States of America

TABLE OF CONTENTS

150

COOLIDGE WALL

WOMSLEY & LOMBARD

1853-2003

ACKNOWLEDGEMENTS

And here it is – an effort to put one hundred fifty years of Cool Law on ice so that it can be preserved for the next one hundred fifty years. This is a history of the law firm (the "Firm") presently known as Coolidge, Wall, Womsley & Lombard, but it is also a book of local history, a history of Dayton people and Dayton business dynamics over the past one hundred fifty years. Because I have had a long interest in the study of family history, I have added a genealogical perspective to discussions of several of the lawyers in hopes that these family relationships will personalize their legal careers and, in some instances, explain the Firm dynamics during certain periods.

The Firm has been very supportive of this project and I thank our Executive Committee, shareholders, associates, administration, and staff for their support. We are all living the Firm's history of tomorrow, and I hope the younger lawyers are taking their notes for the next block of Cool Law.

I have had warm and enthusiastic oral history interviews with my partners Bob Womsley, John Lombard, Roger Makley and Ron Pretekin. The families of former Firm members have been uniformly gracious and helpful. These include the Hugh E. Wall, Jr., family, the J. Bradford Coolidge family (Brad Oelman and Peirce Woodward, grandsons of Brad Coolidge), the Peirce Wood family (Sandy and Alan Johnston, daughter and son-in-law of Pete Wood), the Lee Warren James family (grandson Bill James and his wife Vicki), and the Hiram Strong family (Isabel Frank Vandenburg, the great-granddaughter of Hiram Strong). A number of former members added unique insights from their tenures at the Firm. Bob Matusoff was especially helpful and I appreciate his input.

Special help was given to me from the Dayton & Montgomery County Public Library (Elli Bambakidis), the Germantown Public Library (Robert C. Ammerman), the Montgomery County Historical Society (Bill West, Claudia Watson, and Mary Oliver), The Dayton Daily News (Brad Tillson), NCR, Inc., the archives of Bank One, N.A. (Brad Tidwell, Richard Martin, and Penny Nowak), the Loren M. Berry family (William T. Lincoln and John W. Berry, Jr.), the Dayton Hydraulic Company (Jerv Janney), Bob Crew, Norm Schaefer, Dick Roediger, Joe Schaeff, and Woodland Cemetery.

I must give a special note of thanks to William W. Streeter, an old-fashioned Yankee craftsman who is the proprietor of the Silver Maple Bindery in Northampton, Massachusetts, and a collector and authority on letter copying presses such as that used by the Firm from 1853 until the early 1940s. Bill Streeter showed me his collection of copy letter presses and gave me his time to illustrate how the letter copying process worked.

The cover illustration of the Gunckel Desk was done by my nephew, Kurt Wilberding, a webpage artist for the *Wall Street Journal*. The map sketch of the 1850 Dayton lithograph used to identify certain sites and the floor plan sketch of the Callahan/Gem Savings Building were created by Nick Clemens and Graphics III. Thank you both.

Susan Newhart Elliott (B.A., Miami University, J.D., University of Dayton, M.L.S., Kent State University) from the University of Dayton School of Law provided invaluable research and reference assistance, both in locating information and formulating research strategies. She also did much to improve the structure, style, and language of this book. Thank you. In the Firm's Word Processing Department, I want to thank Elaine Nichols and Sharon Garcia and especially Vicki Thacker who went above the call of duty as she enthusiastically typed countless iterations of text drafts, even at her home while she convalesced from two separate surgeries. Thanks also to Celeste Lane, my secretary, who was a major help to me in the pursuit and organization of my research and illustration materials.

The support and input I have received have been wonderful, but the research, interpretations, and conclusions are mine, and I take full responsibility for any errors of omission or commission. The most recent years of the Firm history are described in only the most basic terms. Their story is still in front of us and better left to a future historian. The history captured here has been selective in its voices and vignettes, but provides, I hope, a seamless continuum of 150 Years of Cool Law.

Merle F. Wilberding

PROLOGUE

During 2003, Coolidge, Wall, Womsley & Lombard is celebrating its sesquicentennial. It is one of Ohio's oldest law firms, with its origins going back to the 1853 partnership of Gunckel & Strong. The Lewis B. Gunckel desk, illustrated above, was used by Lewis Gunckel during his tenure at the Firm and through 1965 was used by virtually every lawyer at the Firm. Upon the death of Joseph Bradford Coolidge, the desk was reconditioned and refinished and then given to Eugene W. Kettering. Upon his death in 1969, Virginia Kettering returned the Gunckel desk to the Firm where it now stands in the Firm's entrance lobby, representing 150 years of legal practice. The succession of law firm names from 1853 to the present is as follows:

1853-1863 - Gunckel & Strong
1864-1872 - Gunckel & Rowe
1873-1876 - Gunckel, Rowe & Gunckel
1877-1894 - Gunckel & Rowe
1895-1899 - Gunckel, Rowe & Shuey

1900-1906 - Rowe & Shuey
1907-1910 - Rowe, Shuey, Matthews & James
1911-1912 - Matthews, James & Matthews
1913-1915 - Lee Warren James
1916-1937 - James & Coolidge
1938-1942 - Coolidge & Becker
1943-1950 - Coolidge, Becker & Wall
1951-1954 - Coolidge, Becker, Wall & Wood
1955-1967 - Coolidge, Wall & Wood
1968-1971 - Coolidge, Wall, Wood & Matusoff
1972-1982 - Coolidge, Wall, Matusoff, Womsley & Lombard
1983-2003 - Coolidge, Wall, Womsley & Lombard

Although the name of the Firm has changed over the years, there are enduring connections among the lawyers of the various generations. Some connections are tangible (and pictured within this book) — including the letter press copying books of duplicate correspondence beginning in 1853, the inscribed books of former partners, and the desk of founder Lewis Gunckel. Some connections are intangible — including the continuing dedication to serving the needs of clients and community. Continuity and a strong communal firm memory have been enhanced by the extraordinarily long, and overlapping, working lives of principals of the firm – thus, current partners Bob Womsley, John Lombard, and Ron Pretekin all worked for Brad Coolidge, Coolidge worked for and with Lee Warren James, and James worked for founder Lewis B. Gunckel. The chapters of this book take their names from principals who established the character of the firm as it endures to the current era. To accommodate the name changes and for convenience of reference, I have used the term "the Firm" to describe the continuing law firm as it operated throughout its one hundred fifty year history.

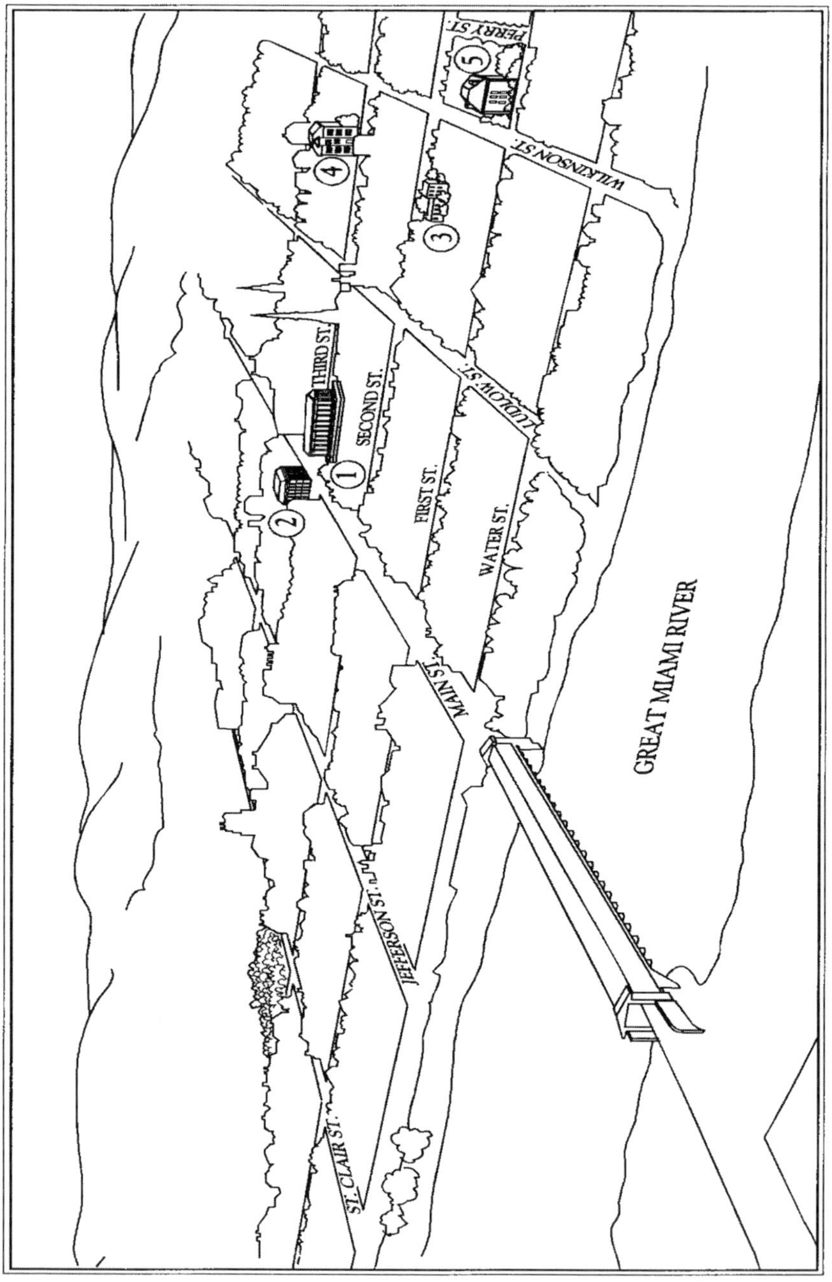
PERRY ST.
WILKINSON ST.
LUDLOW ST.
THIRD ST.
SECOND ST.
FIRST ST.
WATER ST.
MAIN ST.
JEFFERSON ST.
ST. CLAIR ST.
GREAT MIAMI RIVER
1
2
3
4
5

Originally, the term "Cool Law" served as the Firm's formal Western Union cable address as well as the informal team name in Battle of the Business competitions and area softball leagues. When the Internet made its breakthrough into the commercial world, the Firm reserved "Cool Law" in the domain registration process. By 2003, "Cool Law" has become part of the Firm's identity, as our *www.coollaw.com* website continues to grow in cyberspace.

The end papers of this book are from a photograph of an 1850 "View of Dayton" lithograph, drawn from nature and printed in color by E. Sachse & Co. (Baltimore, Maryland). The view is looking south across the Main Street covered bridge and continuing south through downtown and then on to the "Far Hills" of Oakwood in the background. My photograph of that lithograph is courtesy of the Dayton & Montgomery County Library and Isabel Frank Vandenberg, both of whom have originals of the Sachse lithograph. The accompanying schematic map identifies the sites within the View of Dayton which are directly related to the Firm.

1. Court House
2. Conover Building – 1st Firm Office
3. Home of Lewis B. Gunckel
4. Home of Valentine Winters
5. Cooper Female Seminary

The Firm's 150th celebration coincides with two other major historical celebrations in the Dayton community during the year 2003. The State of Ohio is celebrating the bicentennial of its admission to statehood in 1803. The Dayton community is also celebrating through Inventing Flight the centennial of powered flight, recognizing the creative genius of Orville and Wilbur Wright and their aeronautical developments in Dayton both before and after the first flight on December 17, 1903.

CHAPTER ONE

GUNCKEL & STRONG ERA

1853-1900

The story of Cool Law begins, appropriately enough, in ice and snow:

It was winter in southwest Ohio, and it was a cold winter. The snow was crisp and the ground was crusty, leaving the ruts in the road fixed and unyielding. Through this harsh landscape, Lewis B. Gunckel, a student at Miami University, was riding in a stage coach, rumbling down the road from Oxford, Ohio, to his home in nearby Germantown. As he was huddled in the stage coach, he began to shiver. An old dignified passenger offered to share with Gunckel his cloak and blanket to fight the bitter cold. Gunckel later learned that the kind stranger was a well-known and well-respected member of the Dayton bar.

This scene was described by Lewis Gunckel on March 3, 1900, when he was giving a presentation to the Dayton Historical Society and the Montgomery Bar Association on the history of law and lawyers in Dayton. This act of kindness in a wintery cold stage coach by a Dayton lawyer made its mark on Lewis Gunckel and established for him the ideal character of a lawyer, well prepared and attentive to the needs of others. The ideal remained with Gunckel as he became a Dayton lawyer and started a legal practice with Hiram Strong. In 1853 they founded the law firm of Gunckel & Strong, a law firm which would continue under its successors' various names, until now, in 2003, the firm celebrates its 150th anniversary under its present name of Coolidge, Wall, Womsley & Lombard.

The Firm and most of its lawyers during its first fifty years had their roots in Germantown, Ohio, a community in southwest Montgomery County. Germantown was first settled in 1804 by a group of families from Berks County, Pennsylvania. They all met in Pittsburgh and then traveled on river boats down the Ohio River to Cincinnati. They were led by two families -- the Philip Gunckel family and the Daniel Shuey family -- whose lives over the next hundred years would continue to be connected by marriage, community, and business.

The Gunckel family members were millers by trade. To accommodate their trade skills, Philip Gunckel was seeking a location that would provide a site for a mill with good surrounding farm land. He found that site at the fork of the Great and Little Twin Creeks. In 1806, Philip Gunckel started construction of a flour (grist) and saw mill. In one of its redevelopments the mill became known as the Shuey-

Gunckel Grist Mill, reflecting the several family intermarriages.

Philip Gunckel laid out Germantown in a unique plat design that featured diagonal alleys converging in the middle of the block. Probably by no coincidence, Main Street led down to the Shuey-Gunckel Grist Mill. The mill is still standing and has been listed in the National Register of Historic Places. Similarly, the Gunckel Town Plan Historic District with its unique alley design has been designated a National Historic Site.

The settlement of Germantown immediately followed Ohio's admission to the United States in 1803. Ohio's statehood may well have influenced their move from Pennsylvania to Ohio in that statehood might offer a layer of stability for land claims to a new settlement. In any event, Philip Gunckel immediately joined the political process in the new state and was elected in 1806 to represent Montgomery County at the Ohio General Assembly. In 1808, he was re-elected to that post. Then, in 1816 Philip Gunckel was appointed to be an associate judge of the Circuit Court in Montgomery County, a post which he held for the next fifteen years. When he died on May 24, 1848, Philip Gunckel was interred in the Germantown Cemetery, marked with a gravestone recognizing him as the "Proprietor of Germantown."

Philip Gunckel and his wife, Katarina Schaeffer, had eight children, one of whom was Michael Gunckel, born on September 22, 1787. During the War of 1812, Michael Gunckel served first as a captain and later as a colonel, with most of his active duty centered on the forts around Greenville, Ohio. Michael Gunckel married Barbara Shuey, of the other leading Germantown family, and had six children. Five of their descendants would spend part of their careers at the Firm. One of those descendants was their son, Lewis B. Gunckel, who was born on October 15, 1826.

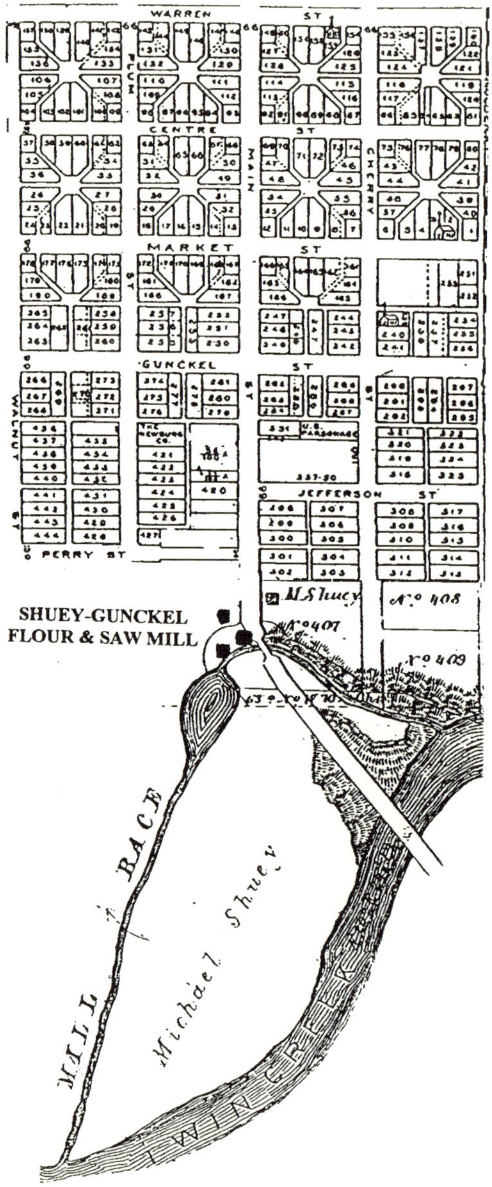
WARREN ST
CENTRE ST
MARKET ST
GUNCKEL ST
JEFFERSON ST
PERRY ST
PLUM ST
MAIN ST
CHERRY ST
WALNUT ST
SHUEY-GUNCKEL
FLOUR & SAW MILL
M.S Shuey
No 408
No 407
No 409
MILL RACE
Michael Shuey
TWIN CREEK

Lewis Gunckel grew up with his family in Germantown. All of the biographical accounts of Lewis Gunckel recite that he graduated from Farmer's College in 1848, and from the Law School of Cincinnati College in 1851. In his 1900 speech to the Dayton Historical Society and the Montgomery Bar Association, however, Lewis Gunckel referred to his years of study at Miami University, with no reference to Farmer's College. Founded in 1809, Miami University would have been an old and venerated school even during Lewis Gunckel's time, although its campus then consisted of only three buildings. It is possible that Lewis Gunckel started at Miami University and was swept up in the "Snow Rebellion" in January 1848. What started out as a student snowball prank became serious when rowdy students barricaded all of the University buildings with snow, preventing teachers and school administrators from entering. In its aftermath, the school dismissed 46 of its 137 students, including eleven of twenty seniors.

It was a tumultuous period for Miami, then a Presbyterian school. The faculty, trustees, and students were deeply divided by religious and political differences that would, on a national level, eventually culminate in a formal split in the church and the Civil War. In 1841, conservative trustees had pushed the popular and highly respected Robert Bishop out of his position as president of the University. By 1845, Bishop and fellow liberal and abolitionist John Scott had resigned from the faculty altogether to join in the transformation of Cary Academy in College Hill (now part of Cincinnati), which had been founded by a Miami alumnus, into Farmers' College (later Belmont College, then Ohio Military Institute, and now the site of Aiken High School). The new college would replace the traditional classical model of higher education with a somewhat more practical

Lewis B. Gunckel
1826-1903

curriculum intended to prepare students for professional positions.

Perhaps Gunckel left Miami voluntarily to follow Bishop and Scott to Farmers' College. Despite the actions of the Miami trustees, ties between the schools were strong because of remaining Miami student and alumni support for Bishop and Scott. At Farmers' College in 1848 Gunckel would have met another student enrolled there because of Bishop and Scott -- Benjamin Harrison, future President of the United States. Then, in 1849, Harrison left Farmers' College to enroll in (and graduate from) Miami, in order to follow Scott, whose daughter he later married. Scott was joining the faculty of a new women's institution in Oxford that would eventually become part of Miami. Regardless of whether Gunckel was expelled from Miami after the Snow Rebellion or left voluntarily, his studies at Farmers' College would have done little to diminish a sense of identity with Miami, and it is probably fair to infer that he emerged from his undergraduate studies with sympathy for Bishop's and Scott's abolitionist and liberal religious convictions.

After being graduated from the Law School of Cincinnati College in 1851, Lewis Gunckel immediately came to Dayton, Ohio, to start his law practice.

During the same period, Hiram Strong grew up in the then rural community of Centerville, Ohio. His father was Dr. Nathaniel Strong, a prosperous doctor. Nathaniel Strong was a native of Northampton, Massachusetts, the stronghold of the Strong family in America. He served as a Naval Surgeon during the War of 1812. Family accounts assert that Nathaniel Strong was a descendant of Governor Caleb Strong, the first United States Senator from Massachusetts, a signer of the United States Constitution, and a patriot permanently remembered with an impressive tombstone memorial in the Bridgestreet Cemetery in Northampton, Massachusetts.

The home of Dr. Nathaniel Strong was located at 34 W. Franklin, Centerville, Ohio. Hiram Strong was born in the original section shown on the right side of photograph. The two-story brick addition was added after his birth and served later as the first public library in Centerville.

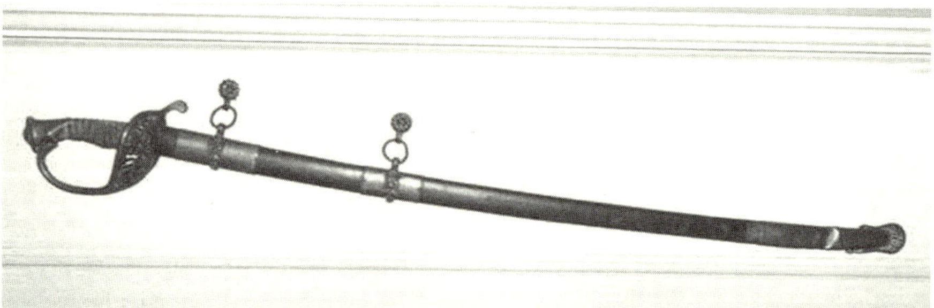

Hiram Strong
Civil War Sword

In 1814, Nathaniel Strong moved to Centerville, Ohio, where he practiced medicine until his death in 1873. During his lifetime, Nathaniel Strong owned a number of houses in Centerville, most on West Franklin Street. His original home was a wooden framed cottage at 34 West Franklin Street. Later, he constructed a two-story brick addition that served as his home and his medical practice office. The two-story brick building later served as the first public library in Centerville.

Nathaniel Strong built other houses in Centerville, one of which is still standing at 63 West Franklin Street. It is known as the Nathaniel Strong House, although it is now oriented to the South (instead of the West) and has been enlarged with an addition or two. The first home, the wooden framed cottage at 34 West Franklin Street, was where Nathaniel Strong lived when he married Hannah Davis on November 7, 1824. In that house, Hiram Strong was born on October 28, 1825.

After graduating from high school, Hiram Strong enrolled at Miami University. He received a Bachelor of Arts degree in 1846, and a Master of Arts degree in 1849. While he was at Miami, he joined the social fraternity of Beta Theta Pi, the first fraternity founded west of the Alleghenies. In the same year, he moved to Dayton and was admitted to the bar in Montgomery County, Ohio.

Hiram Strong soon settled into the Dayton community, joining William C. Bartlett in the practice of law. In Dayton he met Harriet A. Conover, the daughter of Obadiah Conover, one of the earliest and most prominent Dayton settlers. Obadiah and Sarah (Miller) Conover had a large family which included Wilbur Conover, who became known as one of the best lawyers to practice in the Dayton community.

The Conover family was prominent by name and by wealth. In 1811, Obadiah Conover purchased the property

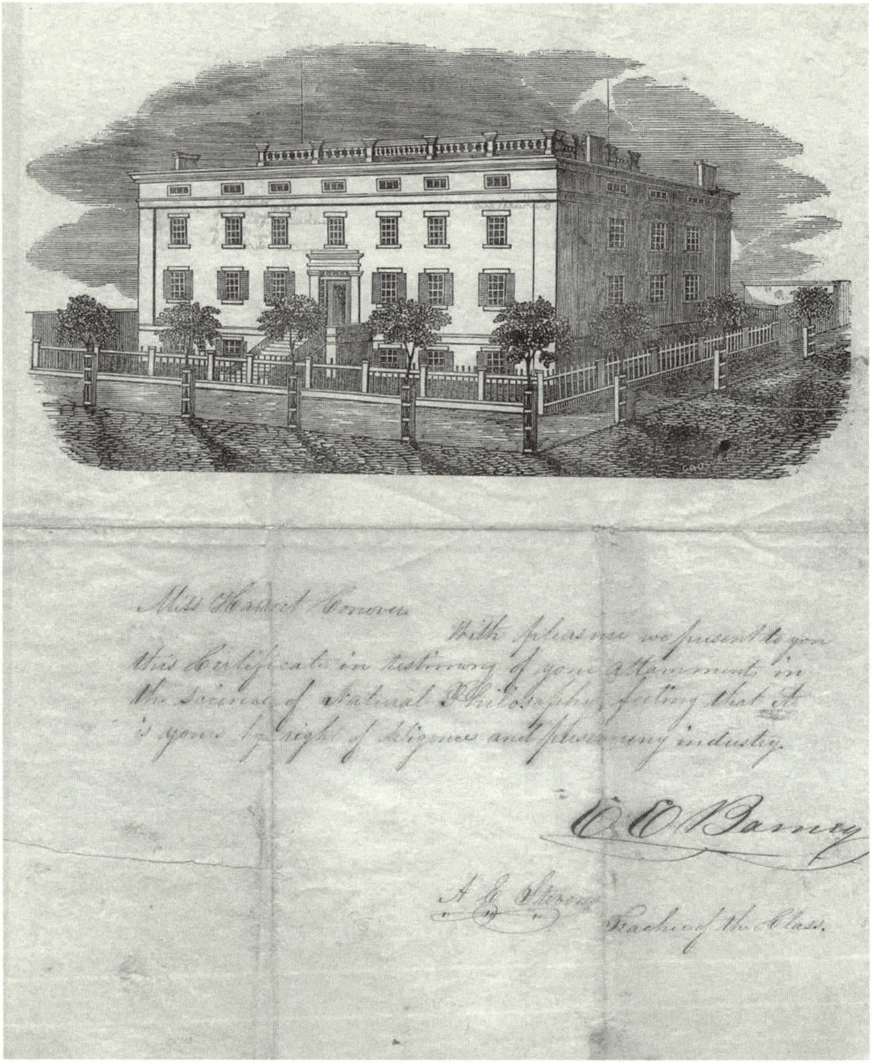

Miss Harriet Conover

With pleasure we present to you this Certificate in testimony of your attainment in the Science of Natural Philosophy, feeling that it is yours by right of diligence and persevering industry.

E. E. Barney

A. E. Strong Teacher of the Class.

Diploma of Harriet Conover (wife of Hiram Strong) dated May 16, 1846, and signed by E. E. Barney on behalf of Cooper Female Seminary. The private girls school was located in a large gray/white building at the southwest quadrant of First Street and Wilkinson Street, Dayton, Ohio.

at the southeast quadrant of Third and Main Streets. Over the years, the Conover family built three succeeding commercial buildings on that property, ranging from an early blacksmith shop, to a four-story office building constructed around 1850, and finally by 1900 the "skyscraper" building then known as the Conover Building, which is still standing but now known as the American Building.

Harriet Conover was born in 1829. On May 16, 1846, she graduated from the Cooper Female Academy (sometimes called the Cooper Female Seminary or Cooper Seminary), a private girls' school started by Robert W. Steele and operated by its principal, E. E. Barney, in a large gray/white building located at the southwest quadrant of the intersection of First Street and Wilkinson Street (the present location of Westminster Presbyterian Church). E. E. Barney signed her handwritten diploma. (He was principal from 1845 until 1849, when he started the Barney-Thresher Company, which later became the very successful Barney & Smith Car Works.)

Harriet Conover and Hiram Strong were married in 1852. They made their home at 361 West First Street (sometimes called 369 West First Street) on property (Lot # 2431 and part of Lot # 2432) Hiram Strong purchased from Thomas Doup on September 10, 1852, in a deed recorded at Book T-2, Page 348, of the Montgomery County Deed Records. There they made their home and had four children: Walter Davis Strong, Nathaniel ("Nattie") Conover Strong, Martha ("Mattie") Strong Gebhart, and Hannah Strong Frank.

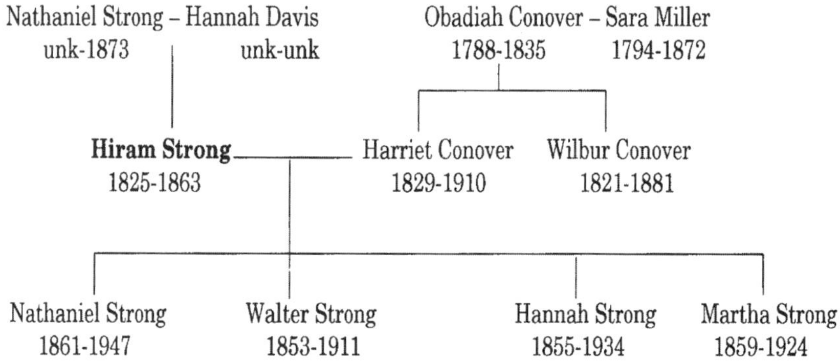

The beginnings of what would become a 150 year professional enterprise may have been in a transaction or two between Hiram Strong and Lewis Gunckel in 1852. We know, for example, that Lewis Gunckel was the notary public for (and perhaps represented) Thomas Doup when Hiram Strong acquired 361 West First Street from him. Shared principles and the mutual respect these two young lawyers had for each other would have encouraged a formal professional relationship. They both had great respect for the law, and they both shared a keen sense of the obligations the law imposes upon lawyers. These character traits, coupled with their inherent and demonstrated integrity, became the underpinnings for their relationship and the law firm they created.

In 1853, Lewis Gunckel at the age of 27 and Hiram Strong at the age of 28 started the Firm under the name of Gunckel & Strong. Reflecting the fact that Hiram Strong was married to Harriet Conover, the Firm located in the Conover Building at the southeast corner of Third and Main Streets, the same building in which Wilbur Conover practiced with Samuel Craighead in the Conover & Craighead law firm. They apparently announced their new partnership as they encountered new clients and new cases. On March 16, 1853, Lewis Gunckel wrote to a referring lawyer in Pennsylvania:

> *Since I last wrote you, I have gone into partnership with Hiram Strong and am now doing business under the name of Gunckel & Strong, to whom you will please hereafter direct your letters.*

The Firm has the "file copy" of this letter as a part of ten volumes of Gunckel & Strong correspondence. The two men were as meticulous in the administration of their law practice as they were in the practice of law itself. They made and kept permanent copies of all of their correspondence. These copies were produced through a unique letter copying press. Indeed, the purchase by Gunckel & Strong of the letter copying press is the first correspondence recorded in their permanent records:

> *Dayton, Ohio*
> *March 8, 1853*
>
> *Jesse A. Willson, Esq.*
> *Cincinnati, Ohio*
>
> *Enclosed you will please find ten dollars for money you have expended in purchasing Letter Press for us. We owe you many thanks for your kindness and shall be glad to reciprocate whenever an occasion offers.*
>
> *Very truly, your friends,*
>
> *Gunckel & Strong*

Photograph of Letter Copying Press.
(Courtesy of William W. Streeter)

Duplicate copies of Firm documents were made by using sequential sheets of a special translucent Japanese rice paper in a letter press copying book which typically was serially numbered, indexed, and bound in leather.

The use of a letter copying press to make the process has been described in *The Origin of Stencil Duplicating* (W. B. Proudfoot) and in *Before Photocopying* (Barbara Rhodes & W. W. Streeter). Bill Streeter maintains a hand bindery and workshop in Northampton, Massachusetts. Streeter, who is a collector of letter copying presses and an authority on copying, identified the Firm's letter copying press from existing copies and popular presses at the time. He has described the process as follows:

1. A letter press copying book consisting of translucent unsized copying tissue (generally rice paper produced in Japan and perhaps brokered through places like Belgium) would be placed on the table or counter top.

2. The book would be opened to the next available blank page.

3. The operator would put a vapor barrier pad below this blank page.

4. The original letter written with copying ink (such as iron gall ink) would be placed on top of this vapor barrier and the blank page would be placed on top of it.

5. Then, the operator would put a damp muslin cloth on top of the blank page intended to retain the copy of the correspondence.

6. On top of the damp muslin cloth would be placed another vapor barrier to protect the previous copies in the book.

7. The original letter would be placed below the blank page so that the iron gall copying ink used to write the original letter would adhere to the bottom of the blank page. This process would be enhanced by the effect of the damp muslin cloth applied to the front side of the copying paper blank page.

8. Once all of these items were inserted, the copying book would be closed and inserted in the letter copying press.

9. The press would be screwed down tight.

10. After one to three minutes, the pressure from the letter copying press would be released, and the copy of the letter could be read

through the front side of the
translucent rice paper.

The letter copy press was used to duplicate all of the Firm's correspondence for almost 100 years, until the translucent paper became unavailable during World War II. The tedious and painstaking process, the least glamorous aspect of legal work, produced an invaluable legacy - a chronicle of the Firm's history. The bound volumes that represent the first ten years of the legal practice remain in the Firm's archives today.

By all accounts, the Firm of Gunckel & Strong prospered and was quickly recognized as one of the leading law firms of Dayton. Their correspondence provides great insights into the nature of their practice and into their character and underlying integrity.

An early letter notes the recent formation of Gunckel & Strong and addresses the Firm's position on payments. This letter disdains a contingency fee arrangement in favor of an expressed preference for "reasonable fee" to be determined after the matter is concluded:

Dayton, Ohio
March 16, 1853

Samuel Goshert, Esq.
Mount Lion, Pa.
* * *
We do not like to make contracts for conditional fees -- we much prefer leaving the matter until decided, and then charging no more than is just and reasonable in the business. But as Mr. Solliday prefers having a contract, we will onsent to do so in the present case. We will,

therefore, undertake the case on the terms named in your letter, viz: If we lose the case we are to receive nothing for our services or for the expenses we have incurred, but if we gain the suit, we are to receive one half of all that is realized in the case -- but with this limitation, that we are to pay all the costs, expense due out of our half of the proceeds. But you say nothing as to who shall pay the costs due, in case we should be unsuccessful. We do not think there is any danger at all -- if we did -- we would not make such a bargain as above. We feel quite certain, we can gain the case -- still there is a possibility of our losing. At least, it is best to provide for any such contingency. Before we can bring suit for a non-resident, we must enter security for costs. Even though we are willing to risk all our time and even our individual expenses, we are not disposed to do any more. If we lose the case -- the costs of court would not probably amount to thirty dollars. Mr. Solliday and wife must agree to pay this -- in case we lose the suit. But as we said before, there is but very little danger -- we feel quite sure, we can recover the property.

Very truly your friend,

Lewis B. Gunckel
for Gunckel & Strong

These records also evidence the long tradition of referring certain matters to other counsel and providing some comfort to them that their legal fees would be paid by the referred client:

Dayton, Ohio
March 10, 1853

W. G. Sellers, Esq.
Troy, Ohio

Dear Sir,

Enclosed please find precipes of two cases, in both of which we wish you retained as associate counsel. Please file the precipes, enter security for costs and see that service is had at your present terms. Our clients are entirely responsible and you need have no fears as to entering security for costs. We will see you soon where we can give you details of the case.

Please answer, whether service will be had at present terms.

Yours respectfully,

Lewis B. Gunckel
For Gunckel & Strong

They were even called upon to aid a young couple who were running away to get married:

3-18-53

Dear Friends:

The Bearer, Mr. George Peckinpaugh of Perry County, Indiana came to me this morning for professional assistance in getting married! The facts of the case are simply as follows: Mr. Peckinpaugh has -- loved not wisely, but too well -- a young lady, of his native country, who is not yet eighteen and whose Father -- being partially insane, objects to her marrying. The Mother and Relatives generally are favorable to the match. Not being able to do anything at home, they determined to run away -- and now that they have started, they don't want to turn back until the "Road that binds two willing hearts" shall be fully tied. From all I can learn of the young man, he is honest and well meaning and desires nothing but what is honorable in the matter. Not being able to get their license here, I advised them to try it in your city. I know "runaways" often get married in Kentucky or on the River, but never knew how. We have not statutes of Kentucky in town -- you have. Advise them as to what is best to be done in the premises -- he has money and is willing to pay you liberally for your trouble.

Do what you can for them -- if at all possible -- get them married. Write me as to your success.

In haste,

Lewis B. Gunckel

P.S. He offered me $40 this morning to get him a license!!

The Firm is fortunate in having materials about one case in which both Lewis B. Gunckel and Hiram Strong worked during their ten year association. In *Joseph S. White v. Rebecca Thomas*, 12 Ohio St. 312 (1861), the Supreme Court of Ohio set aside a verdict of $2,666 in favor of Rebecca Thomas, the Firm's client, and remanded the case for a new trial, at which she won another verdict.

The Supreme Court described the facts as follows: Rebecca Thomas, living in the then rural town of Centerville, alleged that Joseph White had made a promise in August 1857 to marry her, but in breach thereof, Mr. White had married someone else in March 1858. The following month, on April 17, 1858, the Firm filed suit in the Superior Court of Montgomery County on behalf of Rebecca Thomas against Joseph White, seeking damages for that breach of promise. Both Hiram Strong and Lewis Gunckel worked on the preparation of the case, but its trial was delayed by the defendants on several occasions because of discovery and trial preparation issues. On December 10, 1858, the Firm advised Ms. Thomas of the first continuance:

Dayton, Ohio
December 10th, 1858

Miss Rebecca Thomas
Centreville, OH

Madam, your case against White has been continued by White. He swore that a Miss White, I think it was, was absent in Illinois, and that he did not know where she was until it was too late to take her deposition for this term. Yesterday his attorneys gave notice to take depositions at the Office of the Clerk of the County Court at Monmouth, Warren, County, Illinois on Friday, the 7th of this month between the hours of 8 o'clock in the morning and 6 o'clock in the evening. The deposition they expect to take is that of this Miss White. What they expect to prove we do not know. Of that you can best judge. It may be best indeed it would be very well for your brother to go there and be present at the taking of the deposition and get some lawyers there to cross examine the witness. Monmouth is on the Rail Road from Chicago to Burlington and is about 30 miles this side of Burlington. If anyone goes we would like to see them before hand.

Can you tell me exactly where Franklin Russell lives so that we can take his deposition? If so, let us know soon -- here may be another session of the Court in January and we must be ready for trial if possible.

Yours,

Gunckel & Strong

On February 2, 1859, the Firm informed Ms. Thomas that her case was continued again:

Dayton, Ohio,
February 2, 1859

Miss Rebecca Thomas
Centreville, Ohio

Your case against White has been continued today upon the request of White's attorneys. You need not therefore calculate on any trial before next April.

Yours,

Gunckel & Strong

The trial finally went forward in October 1859, and the jury awarded Rebecca Thomas a verdict of $2,666. White appealed to the Supreme Court alleging, *inter alia*, that the jury instructions were erroneous regarding the "reasonableness" of his defense that he discovered facts after he had made the promise to marry that caused him to *reasonably* believe that Rebecca Thomas had been pregnant with a bastard child in 1856. If true, this belief would (under the prevailing law at that time) either excuse his performance or mitigate the damages. (Conversely, if this defense were without a good faith factual basis, the jury could award punitive damages under an *ex delicto* theory, in addition to the compensatory damages under an *ex contractu* theory.)

The Supreme Court decided the case in its December 1861 Term and concluded that the lower court's instructions might have confused the jury on Mr. White's defense and remanded the case for a new trial. A letter dated November 24, 1862, from Lewis Gunckel to a Centerville lawyer named Joseph Kindle indicates the second trial was scheduled to begin about a year after the date of the Supreme Court's decision: "The case of Thomas vs White is set for trial on Saturday, December 6th." By this time, however, Hiram Strong was unable to participate in the second trial because, as will be discussed, he was serving in the Civil War.

It is clear that Rebecca Thomas received another judgment in her favor at that second trial, but there are no records of the amount of the verdict. There is a very telling exchange of correspondence between Lewis Gunckel and Hiram Strong on this case in the summer of 1863. On July 8, 1863, Lewis Gunckel wrote Hiram Strong a long letter which contains the following passage:

> *You know of the result of the Thomas vs White case, but I will have some things to tell you about it when we meet. He [Joseph S. White] paid the judgment without levy. Craighead [Law Firm of Conover & Craighead which included Wilbur Conover, a brother-in-law to Hiram Strong] issued the execution and drew the money. He [Samuel Craighead] did come in to ask about our fee, but when we commenced to talk about it, I found, he had no conception of our position and labours in the case. He thought our labours about equal up to the last trial. although he knew you had commenced and prepared the case, that both of us had helped try it and you had prepared the brief [to the Ohio Supreme*

Court]. I insisted on $500 for our fee. He thought it too much, but wanted $700 himself. I told him as he had the money, he could retain what he pleased, so he paid us $500, which he finally did. Becky [Rebecca Thomas] afterwards paid $ 100 for . . . .

Hiram Strong was sympathetic in his response, written from the Tullahoma, Tennessee, battlefield and dated July 17, 1863:

I was somewhat surprised at the division of the fee in the Thomas case. It looks to me like great illiberality. True neither of us was present at the last trial, but certainly what we did at the first trial should have entitled us at least to half the fee.

The dollar amounts at issue in *White v. Thomas* seem low, of course, due to the rigors of inflation over the last one hundred fifty years, but the expressions of concern in the Gunckel - Strong correspondence, about the amount and payment of fees, and about the lack of appreciation for the efforts expended on a client's behalf, serve as reminders that some aspects of legal practice have changed very little over the last 150 years.

After eight years of prosperous practice, Gunckel & Strong was deeply affected by the outbreak of the Civil War in 1861. The Firm's practice necessarily reflected the social and economic fabric of the Dayton community, of the state of Ohio, and in some respects the entire nation. As the war escalated it became increasingly apparent that there would be no quick resolution to the conflict.

On August 5, 1862, Hiram Strong suspended his law practice and volunteered for a three year term in the 93rd Ohio Regiment of Ohio Volunteer Infantry of the Civil War. Strong, like Gunckel, may have been influenced by or sympathized with the abolitionist convictions of Miami professors Robert Bishop and John Scott, whom he must have known from his student days. Although quiet, he was a man of strong convictions, upon which he based his conduct. At the time of his enlistment, he was thirty- six years old, had a successful law practice, and had a wife and four children; yet he left all of that behind him. Friends described his decision as arising not from a desire for glory or adventure but rather from a sense of duty.

The 93rd Ohio Regiment consisted of men from Montgomery County, Butler County, and Preble County. Over nine hundred men mustered into service and were initially encamped on South Main Street on what would later be the grounds of NCR. On August 23, 1862, the regiment departed at full strength -- eleven companies in all -- for Lexington, Kentucky. The regiment was led by Colonel Charles Anderson, another Dayton lawyer, and Lt. Colonel Hiram Strong.

While conditions were certainly better for officers than they were for enlisted personnel, Strong still suffered many of the hardships endured by all war time personnel. Besides the inherent danger of being in a war zone and being directly involved in the fighting, there were the challenges of the living conditions. The food was at times poor, and at other times just unavailable. For a thirty-six year old officer who had been a successful lawyer for more than ten years, the rigorous military life took its toll.

Strong's wartime correspondence, as retained and preserved in the Firm's archives and the Hiram Strong Collection in the Dayton & Montgomery County Public Library, provides some unique insights into the practice of law at the Firm during the Civil War and the experiences of Hiram Strong as he fulfilled his patriotic duty. From Lexington, the 93rd Ohio Regiment marched to Louisville and Nashville, and then engaged in the Battle of Stones River, Tennessee. On February 21, 1863, Colonel Charles Anderson, the head of the 93rd Regiment, resigned for health reasons, stemming from a gunshot wound incurred at the Battle of Stones River. (Anderson was a Dayton lawyer who later became Governor of Ohio.) Effective March 8, 1863, Hiram Strong was promoted to Colonel and put in charge of the 93rd Ohio Regiment. The regiment then encamped at Murfreesboro, Tennessee, and by the summer, was engaged in fighting at Liberty Gap and Hoover's Gap before capturing the city of Tullahoma, Tennessee, on July 2, 1863.

The partnership continued throughout Strong's service with the 93rd Ohio Regiment. He and Lewis Gunckel regularly engaged in updates on clients and fees. In later years, discussions among the Firm's lawyers about accounting and division of fees would be compared wryly to squirrels divvying up the year's walnuts for their own little hoards. Looking back at their correspondence, it appears that attention to walnut gathering began early in the Firm's history. Strong kept running accounts of fees and cash in pocket memorandum books. He had no ability to keep more detailed records while the regiment was on the move, lamenting in a letter dated October 19, 1862, to Lewis

Gunckel, *"I can keep nothing except in my trunk or pocket, and as my trunk is never or seldom out of the wagon except in a regular camp."*

The pocket memorandum book was meticulously kept. When Gunckel informed Strong that his (Hiram Strong's) balance in the bank was $1,350.81, Strong quickly responded in his October 19th letter with his own computation of cash and fees, which would have increased the balance to $2,397.67:

Fees			
	Housatonic Bank	*$ 142.89*	
	John Dodds	*163.97*	
	Mr. Mead	*75.00*	
	Cooper Seminary	*60.00*	
	Barnetts Estate	*25.00*	
	Mrs. Nelson Clark	*50.00*	
	Dibbler, Work & Morse	*100.00*	
	Crampton	*10.00*	
	Mrs. Barnett	*10.00*	
	Henry Neymie	*10.00*	
Brought forward			*$ 646.86*
Add'l Fees			
	Twin Cr. R.R. Case		*100.00*
	Clap Case		*150.00*
	I H Reed & Co. Case		*150.00*
			$1,046.86
Cash			1,350.81
Total			$2,397.67

Based on this accounting, Strong told Gunckel, "I think you are mistaken," but quickly pointed out that it is "money of which there can be no pressing call."

Strong was, moreover, very sensitive to the burden that carrying on the Firm's business alone imposed on Gunckel, especially as practice declined during the economic havoc of the Civil War. In a letter dated March 13, 1863, Strong wrote to Gunckel:

> *I must speak of the next matter -- our business. The understanding I have had, and which I suppose you have had, is that while I am in the army you take to yourself all of the fees of new business, and when we resume together we make a proper distribution of fees from closing my old business by yourself. This I suppose would be satisfactory unless I remain too long in the army in which case it might be unreasonable. . . . If you find it to your interest to dissolve the partnership, although I shall regret it, yet I shall think it right, and consent at once. It is not proper that I should stand in the way of any more fortunate connection you might make.*

An exchange of letters the following year shows no inclination on Gunckel's part to dissolve the partnership despite the poor economic climate and the difficulties of trying to reconcile long-distance efforts.

> *Dayton, July 8th, 1863*
>
> *Col. Hiram Strong*
>
> *I have been intending to write you for some time past, but ever since my return, I have been so busy that I could not well do so. Our courts are all over now, and as there is little new*

business coming in, I shall for several months to come have all the leisure I want. I have succeeded in closing up a good deal of our old business and in getting fees therefrom. . . . .

In settling up claim of Dayton Maltack v. John L. Covey, I found you had collected $106.50 which you had not paid over. I fixed this by charging you with that much money from fees and then paying it.

I find you did not charge yourself with the fees collected while at home. I found $172.89 from Housatonic Bank, $165.50 from Dibbler . . . What did you get from Horton. He paid, didn't he?

If you want any money for your family or for any other purpose, I can furnish it. Let me know if you have any need.

I shall have no trouble doing all the business during the summer, but little as much as anybody else. . . .

Write me & oblige.
Your old Friend,

Lewis B. Gunckel

The postal service during the Civil War was surprisingly swift. Strong must have received this letter within in a day or two, for his response was dated from an Army camp in Tennessee on July 17, 1863.

HQ 93rd Ohio, Camp Reed
Tullahoma, Tennessee
July 17, 1863

Lew,

Your letter of the 8th was handed me today by Lieut. Brown. I must own that with the best intentions I have proved the most negligent of correspondents. I write regularly to my wife. I intend to write often to my father, to you and to Wil Conover, but the fact is my life here unfits me totally for anything outside of my regular routine of military duties. . . .

My family are in no need of money. You can make use of all you get and leave settlement until I return. I thought I had charged myself with all I got when at home. It may be however only in my cash book. The $106.50 acct. for Casey I don't remember anything about, but I presume you are right. The $172.89 Housatonic Bank is right. As to Dibbler Mark & Morse my memorandum book shows $135.55 instead of $165.50 as you have it. I think the margin to my check to Herbert [Weakley] will show what I paid him on that account. That deducted from $500 is what I retained. . . . But I think my cash and checkbook will show it all. . .

Write me again when you can.

Yours truly,

Hiram Strong

Hiram Strong had become the commander of the 93rd Ohio Regiment when Colonel Anderson resigned due to declining health. The rigors of the war also jeopardized

Strong's health, and he considered resigning from the military, but he was concerned about the well-being of his regiment and skeptical about how a resignation would be viewed by the Dayton community. On several occasions Colonel Strong returned home or asked to return home to recover from health problems. On July 23, 1863, Colonel Strong submitted a request for a twenty-day leave of absence to return to Ohio "for the purpose of restoring my health, which has been impaired since our arrival here July 2."

A few weeks later Strong was back with the 93rd Ohio Regiment when they marched through the Cumberland Mountains and fought in the Battle of Chickamauga on September 19, 1863. During the battle, Strong was hit by a "minnie ball," which was a small arms ammunition that had a lethal and shattering impact on its victims. The bullet entered the right shoulder passing downward and backward through his body. The gunshot wound fractured his humerous and may have punctured his right lung. Eventually, he was taken to a military hospital in Nashville, Tennessee, where he had surgery on October 1, 1863. Despite early post-surgery optimism, Strong developed complications and died in the company of his wife, Harriet Conover Strong, and her brother, Wilbur Conover, on October 7, 1863. The next day there was a long editorial in the *Dayton Journal* on the death of Colonel Strong:

Dayton Journal

Thursday, October 8, 1863

- - - - - - - - -

DEATH OF COLONEL STRONG

Col. Hiram Strong died yesterday morning at one o'clock. Another life paid for our country's ransom. Of the many noble men who have lost their lives in this war, there was no better or nobler than Co. Strong. Of a warm, generous, impulsive nature, he never acted without deliberation – never formed an opinion without reflection. He was a just man, and scrupulously honest. Frank, open and fair himself, he despised cunning, deceit and trickery.

As a speaker, he was forcible, not ornate, and strove to convince rather than to please. As a lawyer, there was no safer counsel at the bar – no cause suffered in his hands for want of attention. He despised injustice, and never knowingly took a retainer on the side of oppression. In his professional intercourse, he was kind, courteous and gentlemanly.

He was an only son and leaves an aged father, now nearly eighty, a wife and four small children. How great his loss will be to them, can only be appreciated when it is known that

> during all his married life, he has been in the habit of spending his evenings at home in the midst of the family circle. Here was the center of all his pleasures, and his highest ambition was to minister to their wants and happiness. He cared nothing for distinction and office, but preferred the purer, better and more philosophical enjoyment of domestic life. May that family never want a friend until loyal hearts cease to beat in patriotic bosoms. The memory of Hiram Strong belongs to the loyal men of this nation. Let them cherish it. He gave his life a willing sacrifice for his country. Let his name have an honored place in her history.

The funeral services were held on Columbus Day, October 12, 1863, at the Strong residence, 361 West First Street, Dayton, Ohio. There was an extraordinary collection of family, lawyers, city officials, and Union supporters at the funeral. After the services, a military cortege of some seventy-five horse-drawn carriages accompanied Colonel Hiram Strong from his home to his final resting place at Woodland Cemetery. The Reverend Thomas E. Thomas gave him his final tribute and salute: "Treason dug this grave and patriotism has filled it."

S | 93 | **Ohio.**

Hiram Strong

Rank Colonel, 93 Reg't Ohio Infantry.

Age 36 years.

Appears on

Field and Staff Muster-out Roll

of the organization named above. Roll dated

Nashville, Tenn, June 8, 1865.

Muster-out to date ...., 186 .

Last paid to ...., 186 .

Clothing account:

Last settled ...., 186 ; drawn since $........ 100

Due soldier $........ 100 ; due U. S. $........ 100

Am't for cloth'g in kind or money adv'd $........ 100

Due U. S. for arms, equipments, &c., $........ 100

Bounty paid $........ 100 ; due $........ 100

Valuation of horse, $........ 100

Valuation of horse equipments, $........ 100

Remarks: Enrolled as Lt. Col. Aug 5, 1862. Promoted to Colonel, March 8" 1863. Died of wounds, Oct 17, 1863. Rec'd at Chicamauga Sept 19, 1863

Book mark: ....

F. H. Hall
Copyist.

(360)

Even before the death of Hiram Strong, it was difficult for Lewis Gunckel to meet the demands of the Firm's legal practice by himself while Strong was serving in the military. He served in the Ohio Senate from 1862 through 1865, when serving in the Senate meant that he had to be in Columbus for great periods of time - without the conveniences of the automobile, the telephone, facsimile machines, or, dare it be said, *e-mail*. The Firm needed someone in the office to help with day-to-day operations, so, during the Civil War, Gunckel and Strong enlisted the services of Herbert H. Weakley, a nephew of Lewis Gunckel, to work at the Firm as a clerk. The family chart in this chapter shows the family relationship, and the Firm's correspondence records confirm his work in the office. Sometimes the Firm simply could not keep all pending cases under control.

Dayton, Ohio
February 20 1863

Jas. Morton, Esq.
Springboro, Ohio

Dear Sir

Mr. Strong of the firm of Gunckel & Strong attorneys at law is now in the Army, being Lieut. Col. of the 93rd Ohio Regiment, and Mr. Gunckel of the same firm is in Columbus, Ohio representing this District in the State Senate.

They have directed me to write you of these facts and to inform you that the next term of the Common Pleas Court commences on the 9th of March next – and owing to their absence *you had better get other counsel in your case in that Court.*

Yours truly,

H. H. Weakley
for attys Gunckel & Strong

Although Herbert H. Weakley was later admitted to practice law in the State of Ohio, he did not practice at the Firm. He did go into business and became the president of *The Herald*, a daily newspaper which, after H. H. Weakley's death, became part of the *Dayton Journal Herald* when it was purchased by James Cox and eventually became part of the *Dayton Daily News*.

After the death of Hiram Strong, the Firm was run by Lewis B. Gunckel. In fact, it became a Gunckel family firm, for virtually all of the lawyers who worked at the Firm through 1900 were related to Lewis B. Gunckel. They were all descendants of both Philip Gunckel (1766-1848) and John Martin Shuey (1750-1829), who comprised two of the Firm's founding families of Germantown in Montgomery County, Ohio. This, of course, also meant that all of the Firm's lawyers (except for Hiram Strong) from its founding through 1900 had deep roots in Germantown, Ohio.

In 1864, another nephew of Lewis Gunckel came to the Firm to study the law under his uncle's direction. Edward L. Rowe, the son of Daniel J. Rowe and Elizabeth Gunckel Rowe, was born in Germantown on September 21, 1842. He graduated from Miami University at Oxford, Ohio, in 1864 and immediately worked under Lewis Gunckel to learn the academic and practical sides of the legal profession. In 1866, Edward Rowe passed the bar examination and was admitted to practice law in the State of Ohio. Not long afterwards, the two entered into a partnership and remained partners with each other (and, from time to time, with others) until Lewis Gunckel's retirement in 1900.

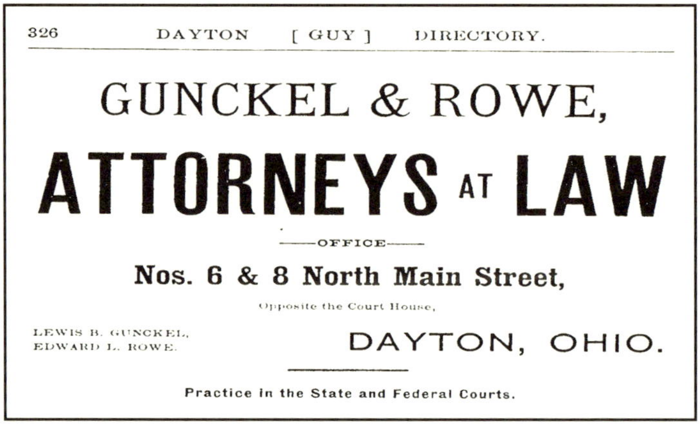
326 DAYTON [GUY] DIRECTORY.

GUNCKEL & ROWE,

ATTORNEYS AT LAW

—OFFICE—

Nos. 6 & 8 North Main Street,

Opposite the Court House,

LEWIS B. GUNCKEL,
EDWARD L. ROWE.

DAYTON, OHIO.

Practice in the State and Federal Courts.

Not long after Edward Rowe came to the Firm, still another Lewis Gunckel family member joined them. Webster W. Shuey was also born in Germantown, on March 11, 1849. He was the son of William A. Shuey and Elizabeth Gunckel Shuey, the grandson of Henry Shuey and Philip D. Gunckel, and the great-grandson of Philip Gunckel and John Martin Shuey.

Webster W. Shuey was doubly related to Lewis B. Gunckel. From a genealogical perspective, Webster Shuey was a first cousin, once removed, of Lewis B. Gunckel because (1) Philip D. Gunckel and Michael Gunckel were brothers, and (2) Henry Shuey and Barbara Shuey (Lewis Gunckel's mother) were brother and sister. The William A. Shuey family had moved from Germantown to Dayton in 1851, so Webster Shuey grew up in Dayton and attended its schools. Later he attended Harvard Law School for a year before returning to Dayton and continuing his legal education under Lewis

Gunckel. In 1871, Webster Shuey was admitted to practice law in the State of Ohio and joined the Firm.

Webster Shuey came to be regarded as one of the prominent attorneys in Dayton, and his abilities and talents contributed significantly to the reputation of the Firm during the last half of the nineteenth century. His devotion to the practice of law left little time for interests other than his family and his religion. On September 12, 1872, shortly after his admission to the bar, Webster Shuey married Harriet "Hattie" McCain and they had a family of six children. Webster Shuey was active in the Raper Methodist Episcopal church of which he served as a trustee.

In 1873, the Firm added Patrick Henry Gunckel and became known as Gunckel Rowe & Gunckel. Patrick Gunckel was not, as has from time to time been indicated, the son of Lewis B. Gunckel. Patrick Henry Gunckel was a nephew of Lewis Gunckel, the son of Henry S. Gunckel and Sarah Stump Gunckel, and the grandson of Michael Gunckel and Barbara Shuey Gunckel. His patriotic name may have been a combined reflection of his birth on St. Patrick's Day in 1848 and his being the son of Henry Gunckel.

Not much has been recorded about the early life of Patrick Gunckel. There is plenty of historical evidence that his father, Henry S. Gunckel, grew up and lived in Germantown. Henry Gunckel was a prominent member of the Germantown community and represented that district in the Ohio state legislature during the 1840s. After that, Henry Gunckel made his living as a tobacco merchant until his death on February 8, 1873. When Patrick Gunckel was admitted to practice law in Ohio and became a member of Firm in 1873, he was twenty-five years old.

Patrick H. Gunckel, Edward L. Rowe, and Webster W. Shuey were able to provide Lewis Gunckel with the support he needed to continue his practice, and, at the same time, they were able to develop their own practices and reputations. The synergy worked well, and the Firm thrived from 1870 through 1900.

Even as new lawyers became part of the Firm, Lewis Gunckel remained the primary impetus, propelling himself and the Firm into the forefront of business and politics in Dayton, in Ohio, and even nationally. Lewis Gunckel also reconnected to the village of Germantown when he married the daughter of Valentine Winters, a native of Germantown, the founder of Winters National Bank, and a very successful business figure in Dayton in the 1800s and early 1900s.

Valentine Winters, the son of the Reverend Thomas Winters of the Reformed Church in Germantown, Ohio, was born in 1807. He started working in a brickyard in Germantown but later moved to Dayton. On January 1, 1829, he married Catherine Harshman, the daughter of the well-known banker Jonathan Harshman. In 1845, Jonathan Harshman opened the Dayton Bank after being chartered by the Ohio legislature. He appointed Valentine Winters as the bank's first cashier. By 1857, Valentine Winters bought out the Harshman family and brought in his son, Jonathan Winters, under a renamed bank called "V. Winters and Son."

Lewis B. Gunckel's marriage to Catherine Winters took place on November 15, 1860. At this time, the Winters family lived in a large mansion at 130 West Third Street, between Ludlow Street and Wilkinson Street -- standing approximately where the old post office building (now housing the U.S. Bankruptcy Court) now stands. At about the same time, the National Banking Act of 1863 authorized national banking charters. On January 1, 1882, The Winters National Bank was granted Charter # 2604 and opened for business. Its first Board of Directors included Valentine Winters, his son, Jonathan H. Winters, and his son-in-law, Lewis B. Gunckel. Lewis B. Gunckel and the Firm had a close relationship with the Winters National Bank, which would continue throughout the bank's history.

By the late 1800s, Gunckel had moved the Firm's offices from the southeast corner of Third and Main to the Callahan Bank Building - the "old" Callahan Bank Building - on the northeast corner of Third and Main, where Winters Bank was located. One of the elevator operators for the Callahan Building during the late 1800s was an aspiring young poet who peddled his first books to passengers. It may be an overstatement to suggest that the Firm gave Paul Laurence Dunbar his start, but it is likely that Firm members, staff, and clients were among the first purchasers of his poetry.

Throughout his career, Lewis Gunckel's efforts were devoted to his community as well as his business. As a member of the Ohio Senate during the years 1862 through 1865, Gunckel pushed for legislation supporting the Union and the common soldier in the Civil War. He was the author of the soldiers' voting law, which was the subject of some of the correspondence between Lewis Gunckel and Hiram Strong. In a letter dated July 17, 1863, Hiram Strong is obviously aware that the soldiers' voting bill has been passed into law and he asks his partner, Lewis Gunckel:

> *By the way, how are we to vote here? Has provision been made for sending duly authenticated copies of the law to each regiment. This should be attended to as early as possible. Again when the nominations are made, committees should be appointed to inform the regiments of the names of the candidates and the offices for which they are nominated.*

Gunckel also pushed for a bill to create a State Soldiers' Home for Ohio, as well as bills for relief of soldiers' families. When these bills were challenged in the Ohio Senate, Gunckel gave an impassioned speech, arguing:

> *We must fight or pay. We ought to do both. We must do one or the other!*

These efforts gave Lewis Gunckel a national spotlight that was probably enhanced by his position as a Presidential Elector for Abraham Lincoln during the 1864 election campaign. When Congress created the National Home for Disabled Volunteer Soldiers, it appointed an overseeing Board of Managers consisting of thirteen persons, including the President of the United States, the Chief Justice of the United States, and the Secretary of War. Ten other managers were appointed, half of them being military generals. Lewis B. Gunckel was appointed one of the managers and was elected Secretary of the Board of Managers, positions he held from 1866 to 1876.

As Secretary of the Board and as one of the national managers, Lewis Gunckel was in a position to exert great influence on the creation and operation of the national soldiers' homes. He successfully argued that the rich and fertile Miami Valley was an excellent location, and Dayton was selected as the national headquarters of the National Home for Disabled Volunteer Soldiers and the site of its main Central branch. (Additional sites were the Eastern Branch at Togus Springs, Maine, and the Northwestern Branch at Milwaukee, Wisconsin.)

The Dayton site was located about three miles west of downtown Dayton and consisted of some 500 acres acquired on March 26, 1867, for $46,000. Dayton was selected in part because of a donation of $20,000 from the citizens of Dayton, led by Lewis B. Gunckel. The site was served by two railroads and rapidly grew to immense proportions. The residential complex for 4,000 to 5,000 disabled soldiers included living quarters, health care facilities, a chapel, a library, work shops, and entertainment buildings.

As the national headquarters, the Central Branch of the National Home for Disabled Volunteer Soldiers in Dayton became a show place for visitors, and Lewis Gunckel, as National Secretary and local manager, often served as the host. On May 30, 1870, he hosted General William T. Sherman, the General of the Army of the United States. With them on the speakers' platform was Major General Thomas J. Wood, the Commanding General of the First Division of the XXI Army Corps of the Army of the Cumberland during the Civil War. General Wood was also the grandfather of Peirce Wood, who would become one of the key lawyers in the Firm during the 1950s and 1960s. On October 3, 1871, President Ulysses S. Grant, his wife, Julia, and his daughter, Nellie, visited the Soldier's Home in Dayton. With them on the speakers' platform were Lewis B. Gunckel and General Wood.

The Central Branch in Dayton of the National Home for Disabled Volunteer Soldiers continued to be a very popular place for its residents and visitors. Over the years, of course, its character and mission changed as the Civil War veterans died and were replaced by the veterans of subsequent wars. In 1930, the National Home for Disabled Volunteer Soldiers merged into the newly created Veterans Administration, and the Central Branch is now known as the Dayton VA Medical Center.

Lewis Gunckel held national political office as well. From 1872 to 1874, he served as a member of the United States House of Representatives from the Third Ohio District. He served on the Committee of Military Affairs and, in general, focused his efforts on containing government spending.

The Firm continued to prosper during the 1870's, as Edward Rowe, Patrick Gunckel, and Webster Shuey supported Lewis Gunckel's practice and continued to develop their own. There are indications, however, that Patrick Gunckel was restless and unsettled. During the 1870's, Patrick Gunckel had at least five different residences, including living with Lewis Gunckel during his first year at the Firm. At the start of 1874, he boarded at the Beckel House but soon moved to 408 W. Second Street after his marriage to Kathryn Turpin on May 13, 1874. Patrick Gunckel stayed at the Firm for only four years, from 1873 through 1876. After that he opened up his own law office in Dayton for two years and then served as United States Commissioner (the predecessor to the present United States Magistrate) for two years. By 1882, Patrick Gunckel left Dayton and moved to Minneapolis, Minnesota, to continue his career there.

Patrick Gunckel's name appears as counsel in numerous reported federal cases coming out of Minnesota and the upper Midwest from 1887 through 1905. These cases indicate that Patrick Gunckel was a talented lawyer who successfully developed a specialization in patent and trademark litigation, most of which involved saw mills and flour mills -- perhaps a continuing reflection on his heritage and interest in the Gunckel-Shuey grist mill and saw mill in Germantown, Ohio. Almost all of his patent infringement cases concerned equipment used in saw mills (*e.g., Torrent v. Duluth Lumber Co.,* 30 F. 830 (D. Minn. 1887), *Rehearing Denied*, 32 F. 229 (D. Minn. 1887); *McEvilla v. Hall & Shelvin Lumber Co.*, 43 F. 139 (D. Minn. 1890); *Wickes v. Lockwood*, 65 F. 610 (D. Minn. 1895); *United Iron Works v. Smith*, 69 F. 827 (8th Cir. 1895).

Patrick Gunckel obviously knew his way around the courtroom, both substantively and procedurally. In 1904, he authored a book entitled *Taxation of Costs in Federal Courts.* It should be noted that it is not a tax book, since it had been written years before enactment of the income tax authorized by the Sixteenth Amendment to the United States Constitution. In the preface, Patrick Gunckel describes the book as a compilation of memoranda he had submitted to judges throughout his career on the questions of what items are recoverable as costs and who should pay them. This book can still be found in Ohio law libraries at the Supreme Court, Capital University, and the University of Akron.

Patrick Gunckel died in Ashby, Minnesota, on September 7, 1910, and was interred at Lakewood Cemetery in Minneapolis, Minnesota. Years later his widow, Kate, and his two daughters, Jeannette and Kathleen, followed him to Lakewood Cemetery.

Meanwhile, Lewis Gunckel had risen to the top of the legal profession in Dayton. Like most prominent business people at the time, he lived downtown. The 1880 Census indicates that Lewis Gunckel was living at 121 West Second Street in downtown Dayton with his wife, Catherine, and three of their children, Kittie, Percy and Lewis Winters Gunckel. In addition, the census listed Margaret Whaley and Mary Horstman, as two servants residing with the family, as would have been common in upper middle class households at that time.

458 DAYTON [GUT] DIRECTORY.

GUNCKEL, ROWE & SHUEY,

Attorneys at Law,

Nos. 6 and 8 North Main Street,

DAYTON, OHIO.

Lewis Gunckel always remembered his Germantown roots. In his later years, as his public life was receding, he concentrated on his law practice and on other charitable interests. Charlotte Reeve Conover described Lewis Gunckel in *Some Dayton Saints & Prophets,* a 1907 book which attempted to preserve the flavor of some of her friends who had been leaders in the Dayton community:

> He was a man of studious habit, a lover of books and pictures. His birth-place Germantown,

> Ohio, benefited by these tastes in the gift of a fine library, solicited for and contributed to by him.

Lewis Gunckel did have help in starting this first library in Germantown. His partner in the endeavor was Dr. John Robertson, a part-time physician and part-time politician. In 1887, after the voters of Germantown turned down a library levy that had been on the ballot, Gunckel and Robertson started their own library campaign and began soliciting contributions. Lewis Gunckel opened up the development fund with a $500 contribution and then succeeded in getting his father-in-law, Valentine Winters, (the head of the Winters National Bank) to contribute $1,000. Together, Valentine Winters and Lewis Gunckel spearheaded the fundraising campaign that produced the first library and the inspiration for all later additions to the library. Lewis Gunckel still has a special place in the Germantown Public Library. The local history room displays, as a memorial to Gunckel, a small roll top desk that was a gift in 1878 to Lewis B. Gunckel in thanksgiving for his contributions to the Soldiers Home in Dayton, Ohio.

These were the grand years for Lewis Gunckel. He was successful in his own right, and he and his wife, Catherine, enjoyed the beneficence of her father, Valentine Winters. In *A Sketch of the Winters Family*, Jonathan Harshman Winters describes the grand dinner party Valentine Winters hosted on March 1, 1888, when he gave each of his children almost $100,000 (almost $2,000,000 in today's dollars.) It appears that Gunckel used some of his wealth to enjoy winters in warmer climate. Jonathan Harshman Winters notes in the same book that Lewis and Kate Gunckel missed a major Winters family wedding --

Valentine Winters, Jr., and Helen Clegg -- because the Gunckels were spending the winter in Southern California.

Besides sharing his wealth with his family, Lewis Gunckel also spent his final years sharing his accumulated knowledge and experience with a new generation of Dayton lawyers, giving presentations to the Montgomery Bar Association and the Dayton Historical Association.

DAYTON [RUB] DIRECTORY. 1115

ROWE & SHUEY,

ATTORNEYS AT LAW

Nos. 6 and 8 North Main Street,

DAYTON, OHIO.

After almost 50 years of service, Lewis Gunckel gave up the practice of law, and the 1900 Census lists Lewis Gunckel as a "retired lawyer" living in the First Ward at 121 West Second Street in the City of Dayton with his wife, Catherine Winters Gunckel and their daughter, Katherine Gunckel. In 1900, the Firm name was changed to Rowe & Shuey, although the *Williams City Directory* continued through 1902 to list Lewis B. Gunckel as a lawyer at 6 North Main Street, suggesting that he had a continuing presence in the Firm. Lewis B. Gunckel died on October 3, 1903. His widow, Catherine Winters Gunckel, lived for ten more years, dying on August 12, 1913. They are both interred in the Valentine Winters plot in Woodland Cemetery, Dayton, Ohio.

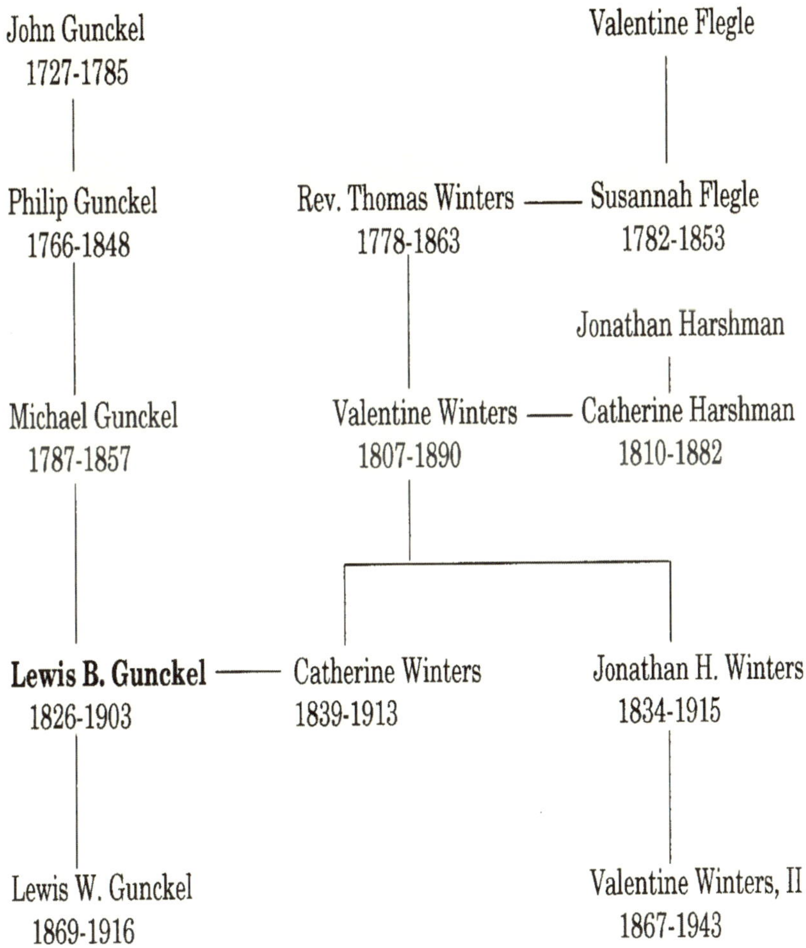
John Gunckel
1727-1785
Philip Gunckel
1766-1848
Michael Gunckel
1787-1857
Lewis B. Gunckel
1826-1903
Lewis W. Gunckel
1869-1916
Valentine Flegle
Rev. Thomas Winters
1778-1863
Susannah Flegle
1782-1853
Jonathan Harshman
Valentine Winters
1807-1890
Catherine Harshman
1810-1882
Catherine Winters
1839-1913
Jonathan H. Winters
1834-1915
Valentine Winters, II
1867-1943

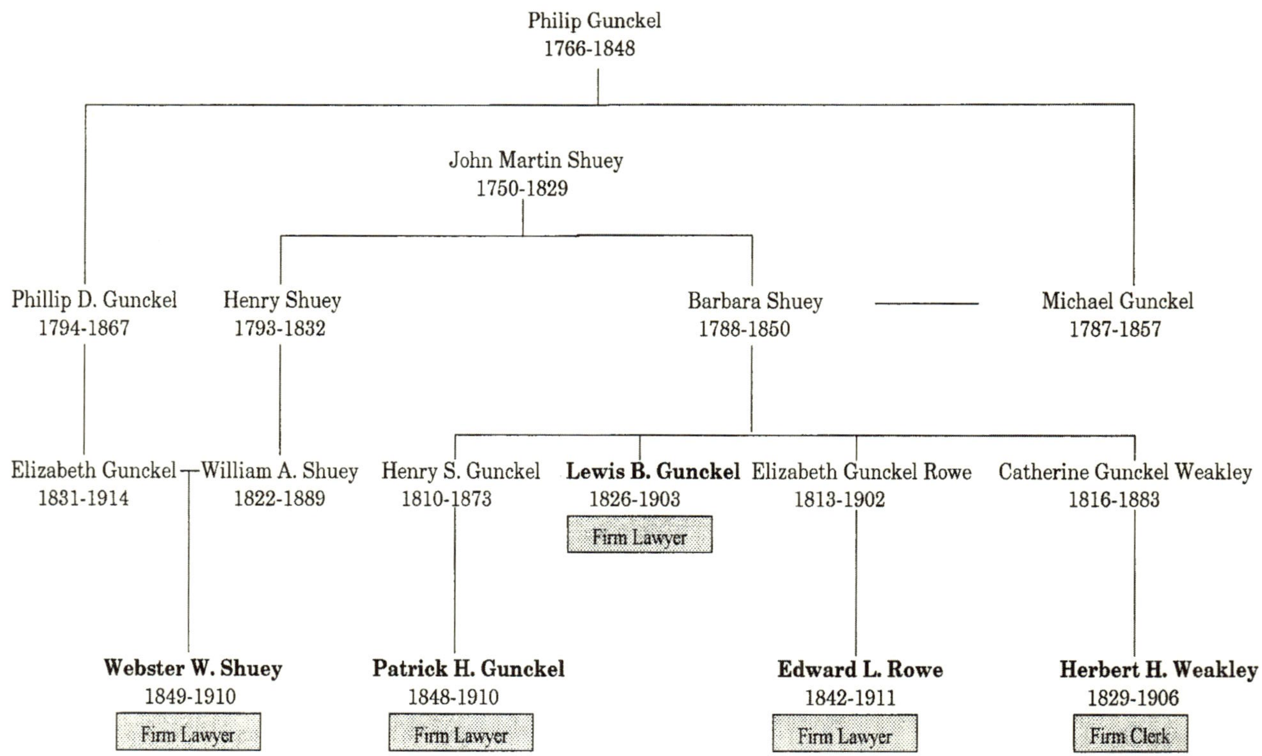
Philip Gunckel
1766-1848
John Martin Shuey
1750-1829
Phillip D. Gunckel
1794-1867
Henry Shuey
1793-1832
Barbara Shuey
1788-1850
Michael Gunckel
1787-1857
Elizabeth Gunckel
1831-1914
William A. Shuey
1822-1889
Henry S. Gunckel
1810-1873
Lewis B. Gunckel
1826-1903
Firm Lawyer
Elizabeth Gunckel Rowe
1813-1902
Catherine Gunckel Weakley
1816-1883
Webster W. Shuey
1849-1910
Firm Lawyer
Patrick H. Gunckel
1848-1910
Firm Lawyer
Edward L. Rowe
1842-1911
Firm Lawyer
Herbert H. Weakley
1829-1906
Firm Clerk

CHAPTER TWO

THE LEE WARREN JAMES ERA

1900-1937

With the turn of the century came a turn in the affairs of the Firm. Lewis Gunckel was semi-retired. Edward Rowe and Webster Shuey were in their sunset years. The new century would bring a new generation of lawyers to the Firm, most significantly represented by Lee Warren James, who was destined to be a major figure both in the Firm and in the Dayton business and legal communities.

In June 1900, Lee Warren James was admitted by examination to practice law in the State of Ohio. Born September 12, 1877, he was only twenty-two years old at the time of his bar admission. He had not been to law school, or even college. Instead, after first growing up on a farm in Montgomery County, he moved with his parents, Wayland P.

and Catherine James, to the city of Dayton. Wayland James was listed in the 1880 Census as a blacksmith and in the 1890 *Williams' Dayton City Directory* as the proprietor of the Southern Ohio Sale Stables and a Dealer in Fine Roadsters and Heavy Draught Horses, at 14 North Valley Street in Dayton. Later, Wayland P. James went into real estate.

Lee Warren James graduated from Steele High School in 1896. Instead of going to college, Lee Warren James set his sights on becoming a lawyer by studying law directly. He studied from 1896 to 1900 under the direction of Oscar M. Gottschall, who was considered one of the premier corporate lawyers in the Dayton community. Gottschall had been admitted to practice in 1866, after having served in the Civil War. Like Hiram Strong, Gottschall was wounded at the Battle of Chickamauga; unlike Strong, Oscar Gottschall recovered from his injuries. He then pursued the highly successful legal career that Hiram Strong might have achieved if he had survived Chickamauga. By 1896 Gottschall had developed his legal skills and practice well enough to be an excellent role model and teacher for Lee Warren James.

Teeming with the self-confidence that seemed to propel his entire career, Lee Warren James moved from what was essentially an apprentice position with Gottschall to the then pre-eminent firm of Rowe & Shuey in January 1900 — six months before he had even taken the Ohio bar examination. The *Williams City Directory* lists both Lee Warren James and Lewis B. Gunckel as lawyers with Rowe & Shuey during 1901 and 1902. On April 30, 1901, he married N. Edith Tyrrell.

In 1904, the Firm made another addition to its staff, hiring Bessie Moore as a secretary and clerk. In 1905, the Firm moved from its 6 North Main Street location to Suite 511 in the new United Brethren Building, commonly called the "U. B. Building" (now known as the Centre City Building). Located at the northeast quadrant of the intersection of

The U.B. Building
United Brethren Publishing House
(Presently called Centre City Building)
Northeast corner Fourth and Main Streets
Dayton, Ohio

Fourth and Main Streets, this fourteen-story office building was considered a "skyscraper" at the time. Its first two floors were devoted to commercial uses, and the remaining floors provided one hundred ninety-two rooms of office space.

By April 1, 1907, Lee Warren James had demonstrated the requisite ability, talent, and legal skills to be admitted as a partner in the Firm, under the new name Rowe, Shuey, Matthews & James.

ROWE 994 ROWE

ROWE, SHUEY, MATTHEWS & JAMES,

ATTORNEYS AT LAW,

509 to 516 U. B. Building,

DAYTON, OHIO.

The next ten years would bring with them a continuing shifting in the structure of this partnership. Webster W. Shuey died on February 3, 1910, and Edward L. Rowe died on March 23, 1911. Consequently, in 1912, the Firm was listed as follows in the *Williams City Directory*.

MATTHEWS, JAMES & MATTHEWS,

ATTORNEYS AT LAW,

509 to 516 U. B. Building,

'Phones: Home 2601.
Bell Main 601.

DAYTON, OHIO.

Edwin P. Matthews, the third name partner, practiced with the Firm for a short time before breaking off and becoming one of the first "souls that once were" — a term still used at the Firm to describe lawyers who have left the Firm to pursue careers elsewhere. Edwin Matthews and his son, William Matthews, left the Firm and left the building, moving to the Callahan Bank Building where they started a new firm.

Meanwhile, the Firm continued in Suites 509 to 516 of the U. B. Building and continued its telephone numbers of "Home 2601" and "Bell Main 601." The practice that James had entered under the direction of Rowe and Shuey was now continued by James, supported by the experienced assistance of Bessie Moore and a new lawyer identified as J. B. Coolidge.

Although Lewis Gunckel was now dead, his contributions remained a tangible part of the Firm's work, and Matthews' departure had little effect on the essential conduct of the Firm's business: the law books acquired by Lewis Gunckel were still the foundation of the library and the substantive legal work; documents were still written on the Gunckel desk and then duplicated with the original letter copying press; the client files and the series of copybooks, now representing more than 50 years of legal work, continued to grow.

To maintain the high level of service to the Firm's clients that had always been a fundamental part of Gunckel's vision, James would soon bring other lawyers into the Firm. Notices in the 1913 *Williams City Directory* evidence both Matthews' departure to begin a new legal practice in the Callahan Building and the addition of new lawyers to the Firm.

LEE WARREN JAMES

LAW OFFICES

509 TO 516 U. B. BUILDING

L. W. JAMES
J. B. COOLIDGE
H. A. ESTABROOK

PHONES : HOME 2601
BELL MAIN 601

DAYTON, OHIO.

EDWIN P. MATTHEWS WILLIAM M. MATTHEWS

MATTHEWS & MATTHEWS

ATTORNEYS
AND COUNSELLORS AT LAW

CALLAHAN BANK BUILDING
DAYTON, OHIO

By 1916, Joseph Bradford Coolidge had become a partner with Lee Warren James. James was 39 years old; Coolidge was 30 years old. The Firm continued under the name James & Coolidge, a name which would remain the same for over twenty years. (It is of note that Hugh Estabrook, one of the founders of the Estabrook Finn & McKee law firm worked at the Firm with Lee Warren James and Brad Coolidge during this period).

Shortly after Brad Coolidge became a partner in the Firm, there was another, rather remarkable transformation in Firm personnel that Rowe and Shuey could not have foreseen when they had hired their new secretary in 1904. On June 29, 1917, Bessie D. Moore passed the Ohio bar examination, was admitted to practice before the Ohio courts, and became associated with the Firm. Born on May 1, 1879, in Chillicothe, Ohio, Bessie Moore graduated from its high school in 1896 — the same year in which Lee Warren James had graduated from Steele High School. She completed a one year program at the Chillicothe Business College and then worked as a secretary and clerk in her father's law office in Waverly, Ohio, before accepting a similar job with Rowe & Shuey in 1904. In 1920, the Firm posted the following notice in the *Williams' Dayton City Directory*, reflecting the addition of Bessie D. Moore as a lawyer with the Firm:

JAMES & COOLIDGE

LAW OFFICES

509 TO 516 U. B. BUILDING

LEE WARREN JAMES
JOSEPH BRADFORD COOLIDGE
H. A. ESTABROOK
BESSIE D. MOORE
J. Q. A. JOHNSON, JR.

PHONES: HOME 2601
BELL MAIN 601

DAYTON, OHIO.

Caricature of Lee Warren James
Businessmen of Dayton, 1905-1906

Could the woman in the sketch be Bessie Moore who was his secretary from 1904 until 1917, when she took the bar examination and was admitted to practice in Ohio?

Like Lee Warren James, Bessie Moore never attended college or law school, but took the bar examination and was admitted to practice law after years of self-study and training in a law office. She continued to work at the Firm as a lawyer until 1937. Lee Warren James and Bessie Moore had a lot in common, and it appears that they developed and maintained a close relationship through their professional lives. Moore left the Firm in 1937, at the same time that Lee Warren James left. She continued to practice law in her own office in the Callahan Building, where her practice included the representation of Lee Warren James' interests in Dayton. The timing of her departure and her representation of those interests suggest that her departure from the Firm was sympathetically related to the departure of Lee Warren James.

Bessie Moore was one of the first women (if not *the first* woman) to practice law in Dayton. As an acting municipal judge, Bessie Moore is believed to have been the first woman ever to sit on a criminal court bench in Dayton. She was not only the first female lawyer to work at the Firm, she was the only female lawyer to work at the Firm until 1979, when Ann Davidson was admitted to practice. (Like Bessie Moore, Ann Davidson previously worked at the Firm in a support capacity, as a paralegal, before attending law school at the University of Dayton.)

Throughout her years of practice, Bessie Moore was very active in the Dayton community. She served on the Board of Trustees of Antioch College for a number of years, as well as having memberships in a full portfolio of community, arts, legal, and women's organizations. She died on February 1, 1951, at the age of 71.

In 1920, James moved the Firm to the Northeast corner of Second and Main Streets, into a building that became known as the L. T. Cooper Building.

Lee Warren James' legal skills and flamboyant persona evoked special mention from time to time in the local history books, including Reverend A. W. Drury's *History of City of Dayton and Montgomery County, Ohio* in 1909.

> Lee Warren James, a member of the well known law firm of Rowe, Shuey, Mathews & James, of Dayton, does not need introduction to the readers of this volume, for the firm occupies a foremost place in the ranks of the legal fraternity, enjoying the most extensive and important clientage.

James was said to be thoughtful, diligent, and resourceful in his practice generally and in his major transactions and trials specifically. At the same time, he was able to present his cases all the more effectively because of his dynamic personality, his Olympian stature, and his *haute couture* wardrobe. James belonged to the Dayton Country Club where he had a reputation as an excellent golfer. Indeed, when future Firm partner Hugh E. Wall, Jr., was a lad, he used to caddy for James at Dayton Country Club. James left his mark and his photograph at the Dayton Country Club by serving as its President in 1926. Lee Warren James was a

Lee Warren James
1877-1963

powerful and commanding figure who had broad shoulders, a thick-set chest and a Hollywood aura about him. To top off the image, he drove around Dayton in a Rolls Royce, reportedly the first in Dayton.

In fairness to Lee Warren James, the Olympian stature reflected Olympian talent. Although he was best known for his business and corporate talent, James was equally adept in the courtroom. James appeared both in the United States Supreme Court, arguing some extremely difficult cases, and, more successfully, in the Ohio Supreme Court, winning a number of cases addressing a wide variety of issues and areas of law, including disputes about conflicts between the Dayton City Charter and the Ohio General Code (*State ex rel. Lenz*, 90 Ohio St. 305 (1914)), the relationship between liens and sureties (*Boyd v. Royal Indemnity Co.,* 126 Ohio St. 322 (1933)), and charitable immunity (*Waddell v. Young Women's Christian Association,* 133 Ohio St. 601 (1938)).

One of Lee Warren James' United States Supreme Court cases, fairly early in his career, was *Dale v. Pattison* (234 U.S. 399 (1914)), which had its roots, like the Firm, in Germantown, Ohio. James represented the trustees of the David Rohrer Distillery bankruptcy. The Distillery had been opened by Rohrer's father in 1847 as the Mudlick Whiskey Distillery. Rohrer took over operations in the 1860s and expanded to include a brewery (which reputedly produced a "wholesome and nourishing" beer), a large grain elevator, and a warehouse. The Distillery could produce almost 60 barrels of whiskey a day, and his warehouses held almost 20,000 barrels of whiskey and other spirits. In 1909 Rohrer and the Distillery were adjudged bankrupt, and a dispute arose as to rights to the barrels of whiskey in the warehouse.

The trial court ruled in favor of the trustees, but the United States Supreme Court (whose panel then included the great Oliver Wendell Holmes, Jr.), in a lengthy (for the time) opinion that reflected the complexity of the issues, eventually held in favor of a creditor who claimed his own rights were superior. Nonetheless, the case established Lee Warren James as a lawyer capable of handling the most difficult cases.

Complicated and lucrative business transactions became James' primary forte. He had the requisite legal knowledge and, with that, the intuition and instincts of a very sharp businessman who knew when and how to close the deal. Certainly the business environment played an important role in James' success. His work in the Firm brought him close to the Winters family, and then to John Patterson, the founder of the National Cash Register Co. (later called "NCR") and to Charles F. Kettering. Considered in his time to be the premier corporate lawyer in the city of Dayton, Lee Warren James sat on the board of directors for a large number of public and private corporations, including Winters National Bank, and Mutual Home & Savings Association.

On the Winters Bank board, Lee Warren James sat with Frank Hill Smith and Valentine Winters II. All of these men had reached the pinnacle of success in the Dayton business community. Valentine Winters II was the grandson of the Valentine Winters, the founder of Winters National Bank and the father-in-law of Lewis B. Gunckel, the founder of the Firm. Frank Hill Smith was the head of Frank Hill Smith, Inc., a builder of a large number of downtown Dayton buildings, including thc 1921 Winters Bank Building, the First Street Garage, and the Dayton Art Institute. Frank Hill Smith also headed the Dayton Hydraulic Company, which had been created by an act of the Ohio legislature on March 6, 1845, making it the oldest corporation in the State of Ohio that is still operating today.

By the early 1920s, the three major shareholders of the bank were the Winters family, Frank Hill Smith, and C. E.

1921 Board of Directors of Winters National Bank

Clockwise from left front: F. B.Currigan, R. R. Dickey, Howard F. Marston, Lee Warren James, Valentine Winters, Frank Hill Smith, Joseph Herzstom, S. Rufus Jones, Ezra F. Kimmel and Russell Tompert.

Burnett. Winters Bank had approximately ten million dollars in deposits. Then, on October 10, 1924, a major transaction occurred. By all accounts, the Winters Bank was in trouble and it sent an emissary to Charles F. Kettering, the world famous inventor ("Boss Ket"), who was then a Vice-President of General Motors. Boss Ket responded by buying all of the Winters' family bank stock and, in addition, injected new capital into the bank. With that transaction, Charles F. Kettering became the Chairman of the Board and the Kettering family became the controlling shareholder of Winters Bank for the next sixty years, ending with its eventual merger into Bank One, N.A., in 1983. Lee Warren James continued the Firm's representation of Winters Bank through the transfer of control from the Winters family to the Kettering family and, in the process, further strengthened the Firm's relationship with Winters Bank.

In a separate highly significant corporate transition, Lee Warren James helped to transform the National Cash Register Co. from a closely held company to a publicly held company. When John Patterson founded the National Cash Register Co., he structured it as an Ohio corporation. All of its stock was held by the Patterson family, but there was a profit-sharing system for the benefit of the employees, a system that distributed an average of $2,000,000 per year to the employees from1921 through 1925. When Patterson decided to reorganize NCR as a publicly held company, James was one of four individuals involved in the business side of the transaction:

Frederick Beck Patterson	President
John H. Barringer	Vice President
Stanley Charles Allyn	Comptroller
Lee Warren James	Outside Counsel

Those four individuals (called "Patterson and his Associates" in the literature) bought the entire outstanding common stock of the old Ohio corporation and then organized a new Maryland corporation, National Cash Register Co., which would have two classes of common stock and a board of eleven directors. In one of the court cases arising from the reorganization (*McQuillen v. National Cash Register,* 27 F. Supp. 639 (D. Md. 1939)), the Court suggests that Lee Warren James may even have been a director.

The underwriter for the public offering was Dillon, Read & Co., an established investment banking firm now part of SBC Warburg Dillon Read. Patterson and his Associates agreed to sell to Dillon Read all but 382,438 shares of Class B stock. Patterson and his Associates received $40 Million in cash. The transaction became effective on January 2, 1926.

The public offering is described in *National Cash Register Co. v. United States*, 10 F. Supp. 687 (Ct. Claims 1935). The case arose out of National Cash Register's efforts to claim an income tax deduction for cash payments the company had made to a trust which was commonly accepted by the employees to be a continuation of the old company's profit sharing plan. In years 1921 through 1925, the company had deducted without challenge from the Internal Revenue Service its $2,000,000 annual distribution to the profit sharing plan. After the reorganization, the company continued to make distributions in about the same amounts to the profit sharing system, and continued to claim a corporate tax deduction for these payments.

Subsequently, the Internal Revenue Service disallowed these deductions. It asserted that the structure of the profit sharing system was now critically different because the trust comprising the new profit sharing system was actually a trust holding 150,000 shares of Class B that had been contributed by Patterson and his Associates out of the 382,438 shares they had retained in the transaction. The Internal Revenue Service successfully took the position that the new profit sharing system had been created entirely by Patterson and his Associates and that the corporation had contributed nothing to the plan. Therefore, National Cash Register Co. could not claim an income tax deduction for the annual profit distributions.

In the course of its opinion, the Court of Claims observed that Patterson and his Associates had derived personal profit of approximately $14 million out of the $40 million paid by Dillon Read for the stock resold in the public offering. As the court went on to note, "[T]he profits of Patterson and his Associates accrued to them personally and individually and were not turned over to or participated in by" National Cash Register Co. In other words, it was a secondary stock offering for the primary benefit of the selling shareholders, not the corporation.

The opinion does not recount how the profits were allocated among Patterson and his Associates, but it does set forth the relative percentages of stock contributed by each individual to the new profit sharing trust. The court noted that 150,000 shares had been contributed to the new profit sharing trust by Patterson and his Associates in the following proportions:

Frederick Beck Patterson	116,667 Shares
John H. Barringer	11,111 Shares
Stanley Charles Allyn	11,111 Shares
Lee Warren James	11,111 Shares
Total	150,000 Shares

Patterson, of course, contributed the largest portion – almost 80%. His Associates each contributed portions of approximately 7%. If Lee Warren James' percentage in that aspect of the transaction applied to the allocation of the total $14,000,000 net profit earned by Patterson and his Associates, James' share in those net profits would have been $1,037,026. It has also been reported that Homer Snyder, the then Treasurer of National Cash Register, signed a $1,000,000 check to Lee Warren James in connection with the legal work in taking the company public. In keeping with his Hollywood aura, Lee Warren James sprinkled some of his new wealth among the rank and file, both at the Firm and at National Cash Register, startling and delighting a janitor or two along the way.

By 1935, the Firm had also added Charles Brennan (LL.B., University of Dayton) and Phil Becker (Denison University and LL.B., Washington & Lee University). The Firm was still in the L. T. Cooper Building at the northeast corner of Second and Main Streets, but it had changed its telephone number from MAin 1000 to ADams 8177. When telephone numbers in Dayton were increased from six digits to seven digits, a "2" was added to the front of the number, making it BAldwin 3-8177 (223-8177), the Firm's present telephone number.

LAW OFFICES

JAMES & COOLIDGE

N. E. COR. MAIN AND SECOND STREETS

DAYTON, OHIO

LEE WARREN JAMES
JOSEPH BRADFORD COOLIDGE
BESSIE DAVIS MOORE
THOMAS WARREN JAMES
CHARLES EDWARD BRENNAN
PHILIP ROHRER BECKER

September 16,1935.

The Firm's 1935 Martindale-Hubbell listing indicates that the Firm had added not only new lawyers but also a satellite office at 48 Wall Street, New York, New York, reflecting the extraordinary business relationships of Lee Warren James.

General Practice
Specialize in Corporation Law

JAMES & COOLIDGE
300 L. T. COOPER BUILDING
DAYTON, OHIO
(New York City Office: 48 Wall Street)

Telephone:
Adams 8177

MEMBERS OF FIRM

Lee Warren James, born Montgomery County, Ohio, September 12, 1877; admitted to bar, 1900, Ohio; Washington, D. C. Preparatory education, public schools, Dayton; legal education, law office, Gunckel, Rowe & Shuey. *Member:* Dayton, Ohio State and American Bar Associations.

Joseph Bradford Coolidge, born Holliston, Massachusetts, February 14, 1886; admitted to bar, 1912, Ohio. Preparatory education, Harvard College (A.B., 19[illegible]); legal education, Harvard Law School (LL.B., 1912). *Member:* Dayton Bar Association.

Bessie Davis Moore, born Chillicothe, Ohio, May 1, 1879; admitted to bar, 1917, Ohio. Preparatory education, public schools, Chillicothe; legal education, law offices, Lee Warren James, Dayton. *Member:* Dayton and Ohio State Bar Associations.

ASSOCIATES

Charles Edward Brennan, born Xenia, Ohio, Aug. 7, 1905; admitted to bar, 1929, Ohio. Preparatory education, University of Dayton (B.S.); legal education, Georgetown University and University of Dayton (LL.B.). *Fraternity:* Delta Pi Kappa. *Member:* Ohio State Bar Association.

Philip Rohrer Becker, born Dayton, Ohio, Dec. 27, 1905; admitted to bar, 1929, Ohio. Preparatory education, Dennison University; legal education, Ohio State University, Washington & Lee (LL.B.). *Fraternities:* Beta Theta Phi; Phi Delta Phi. *Member:* Ohio State Bar Association.

What is striking about the listing is how Lee Warren James and Bessie Moore described their "preparatory education," Lee Warren James listed the "public schools of Dayton," and Bessie Moore listed the "public schools of Chillicothe." For their legal education, Lee Warren James listed "Gunckel, Rowe & Shuey" and Bessie Moore listed "Lee Warren James." Here were two Ohio grass roots high school graduates who obtained their entire legal education on the job. Tucked between them in Martindale-Hubbell, and probably tucked between them in Firm dynamics, was Joseph Bradford Coolidge — born in Boston and educated at the prestigious Boston Latin School, Harvard College, and Harvard Law School.

By 1935, Thomas Warren James, the son of Lee Warren James, had come and gone as a lawyer at the Firm. Born in 1901 as the first son of Lee Warren James and Edith Tyrrell, Thomas Warren James, by all accounts, was pushed by his father to Yale University to get the formal education Lee Warren James never had. Parental pressure pushed him to become a lawyer in Dayton and New York, and later a stockbroker in New York.

JAMES AND COOLIDGE

LAW OFFICES

Rooms 300-304 North-east Cor. 2d and Main

LEE WARREN JAMES
JOSEPH BRADFORD COOLIDGE
BESSIE D. MOORE
DANIEL L. DWYER
THOMAS W. JAMES

Associates:
CHAS. E. BRENNAN
PHILIP R. BECKER

DAYTON, OHIO

PHONE MAIN 1000

Thomas Warren James failed to achieve the success that his father enjoyed. He did not love the law as his father had. He did, however, develop the family passion for exotic cars, following his father who in 1927 had the first Rolls Royce in Dayton and his grandfather Wayland James who advertised in 1890 that he was a "Dealer in Fine Roadsters and Heavy Draught Horses". Besides having an interest in fast and exotic cars, Thomas Warren James excelled in golf, winning the club championship at Dayton Country Club in 1925.

When his father established the Firm's office in New York City, Thomas Warren James soon followed him, living on Long Island and attempting to make his mark in the East Coast legal and business world. Once in New York, he rarely returned to Dayton. In 1947, Thomas Warren James accompanied his father Lee Warren James who was taking a busload of business associates to the Kentucky Derby and stopped in Dayton to pick up Thomas James' son, William Lee James. After that trip, neither Lee Warren James nor Thomas Warren James returned again to Dayton. Thomas Warren James died in New York in 1962.

It appears that Lee Warren James had a presence in New York City for some period before 1935. His move to New York was probably precipitated by a number of factors. He had vaulted into the New York investment community with his participation in the initial public offering by National Cash Register. From a personal standpoint, he may have been ready for a change. His first wife, Edith Tyrrell, had died in 1925. Finally, there was the investment factor. According to the James' family history, Lee Warren James established a presence in New York to manage the growing fortune of Charles F. Kettering, the inventor.

James' grandson, William Lee James, then a young boy, remembered being in his grandfather's office at 48 Wall Street on August 15, 1935, where he read the breaking news coming over the ticker tape that Will Rogers and Wiley Post had been killed in a plane crash in Point Barrow, Alaska. The fact that Lee Warren James had a ticker tape in his own office suggests that he was in New York more as an investor and stockbroker than as a practicing lawyer. Moreover, the 1935 Martindale-Hubbell does not list him as a member of the New York bar. All of this is consistent with the theory that Lee Warren James was in New York to manage the Kettering money and, perhaps secondarily, related legal interests.

The concept of a New York branch office of James & Coolidge was less impractical than it might seem. While travel between Dayton and New York during the 1930's may now seem like a slow and tedious experience, his regular commute may have in some ways been more convenient and

"Spirit of St. Louis"
Pennsylvania Railroad

Courtesy of Railroad Museum of Pennsylvania and Pennsylvania Historical and Museum Commission

Spirit of St. Louis
Eastbound train departing St. Louis Union Station
for Dayton, Washington, D.C., and New York
(Courtesy of Rail Photo Service collection of Joe Welsh)

enjoyable than current travel from Dayton to New York City. Lee Warren James would simply drive to Union Station in Dayton and board the "The Spirit of St. Louis," the popular name of the overnight Pennsylvania Railroad train # 30 which ran from St. Louis to New York, complete with dining cars, lounge cars, and sleeping cars. During the evening, he would have a luxury dinner in the dining car and then retire to his first-class sleeping compartment. The next morning he would arrive fresh and rested at Grand Central Station in mid-town Manhattan and take a short taxi ride to his office on Wall Street to deal with the day's legal and investment challenges.

By most accounts, the final departure of Lee Warren James from the Firm in 1937 was predicated in part on a fallout with Joseph Bradford Coolidge over splitting fees — squirrels and walnuts again. Whatever the precipitating incident, James' departure from the Firm was probably inevitable as his efforts were focused more and more on the New York interests, and Coolidge, accordingly, assumed increasing responsibility over day-to-day operation of the Firm. With James' withdrawal, Coolidge began to consider alternate office space for the Firm and finally settled on the remodeled Callahan Bank Building.

As is shown in the accompanying photographs, the original first five floors of the original Callahan Bank Building remained, but a 1919 renovation removed its half dozen or so commercial-Romanesque turrets and mini-towers in favor of an additional seven floors, creating a true office tower in downtown Dayton. The Firm maintained offices on the 11th and 12th floors through 1967. This building was later called the Callahan Building and still later the Gem Savings Building before being torn down in the early 1970s. (When it was torn down, its cupola and clock tower were saved and installed atop the Reynolds + Reynolds Company building on Germantown Street overlooking I-75.)

The original Callahan Bank Building
Northeast corner of Third and Main Streets
Dayton, Ohio

Callahan Building
Gem Savings Building
Northeast corner Third and Main Streets
Dayton, Ohio
This reflects the seven-story tower added
in the 1919 renovation.

When Coolidge began to consider new space for the Firm, both the ninth and twelfth floors of the Callahan Bank Building were vacant. The twelfth floor had just been vacated by the forerunner of Smith & Schnacke, which occupied it for one year before moving to the new Talbott Tower. Prior to that, it had been occupied by George Mead and Nelson Talbott. The twelfth floor was a wonderful office location. It occupied the top floor of an office tower located across Main Street from the court house. Nelson Talbott's office had included a huge Normandy style fireplace. That corner office was immediately claimed by Brad Coolidge. To complete the move, he placed the following announcement in the next *Williams City Directory*.

JOSEPH BRADFORD COOLIDGE
PHILIP R. BECKER
WILLIAM J. BRADLEY

Coolidge & Becker

Law Offices—Twelfth Floor Callahan Bldg.
Tels. Adams 8177-8178

(1939) WILLIAMS DIRECTORY CO.'S

True to his nature, Lee Warren James went out of the Firm and out of Dayton in grand style. He moved to New York City at the age of 60 and the office there became his own. In Dayton, he did maintain an official, if not personal presence. Lee Warren James and Bessie D. Moore, whose mentor he had been, joined forces and took the space in Suite 902 of the Callahan Bank Building. Thus James maintained a nominal presence in Dayton, perhaps because Ohio was the only state in which James was licensed to practice law, but it appears that Bessie Moore actually handled most of his remaining Dayton legal interests when local attention was required. At the time of his departure from the Firm, Lee Warren James sold his grand residence at 630 Runnymede in Oakwood and fixed his residence in New York City.

One of the cases involving Lee Warren James that lingered after his departure from Dayton and produced an interesting comment on his circumstances was *Mutual Home & Savings Ass'n v. Merion*, 37 N.E.2d 109 (Montgomery Cty Ct. Appeals 1941). In its early years, Lee Warren James had served as attorney and director for this building and loan association. In 1939, the association was engaged in a liquidation plan in which certain assets (including mortgage notes) were sold and the proceeds delivered to an escrow agent who, in turn, used those funds to buy stock of the association in the open market. Although some form of escrow plan had been previously accepted by the Superintendent of Building & Loan Associations in other liquidations, the Mutual Home plan was, in the view of the Superintendent, far beyond the scope of any escrow plan previously sanctioned.

There was a bitterly contested fight between the board of directors and the Superintendent over who had control over the liquidation plan. The Common Pleas Court of Montgomery County ruled that the Superintendent had exceeded his authority when he issued an order setting aside the directors' plan. The Bill of Exceptions to this order contained more than four thousand pages – some indication of the intensity of the dispute.

At the heart of the controversy was the Superintendent's refusal to approve the "James Deal," a proposed transaction involving a mortgage "on a very valuable lot on Main Street" owned by Lee Warren James who was described as a "very prominent lawyer in the city of Dayton, now residing in New York City." The court noted that, "aside from his real estate holdings, Mr. James had no other known assets," although the Superintendent's objection was unrelated to James' finances. The Court of Appeals reversed the decision of the lower court and approved the taking over of the association's liquidation by the Superintendent of Building & Loan Associations.

In 1949, twelve years after he left Dayton, Lee Warren James again appears on behalf of Dayton clients, this time the owner of the designs, specifications and patents for a bombsight. The owner was pursuing a claim against the United States because the U.S. Air Corps at Wright Field had provided the client's materials to NCR for its use in producing 20,000 bombsights in 1941 (*Estoppey v. United States,* 83 Supp. 840 (Ct. Claims 1949)). The Government argued that the relevant statute permitted compensation only for "components" of an aircraft and a bomb sight was an aircraft "accessory." The U.S. Court of Claim ruled in favor of James' client, holding in a classic understatement that a bombsight was more than a convenience or an accessory to a bomber.

Lee Warren James was not only a lawyer and manager of investments, but a leading investor in a variety of companies. In Dayton, he was President of the Day-Fan Electric Company, until it was acquired by General Motors

Corporation in 1929, and President of the Dayton Country Club. Later, in New York, he was President of the George Washington Life Insurance Company.

James was also President of the Metropolitan Club of New York, which was located on Fifth Avenue at 60th Street, overlooking the Plaza Hotel and Central Park. He has been noted as being the only person to serve as President of the Metropolitan Club in two unconnected terms. In 1950 James was honored by the Metropolitan Club with a special Testimonial Dinner. He had played such a big role in the preservation of the Club that the Tap Room on the second floor was renamed the "Lee Warren James Room." In it hangs an oil portrait of Lee Warren James by Howard Chandler Christy (1873-1952), a famous painter first known as an illustrator (for such books as *The Lady of the Lake* by Sir Walter Scott and *Evangeline* by Henry Wadsworth Longfellow and for magazines such as *Harper's* and *Scribner's*.)

Eventually, James moved into the Metropolitan Club where he died in June 1963. There were many stories that, between highly speculative investments, fluctuating markets, and a taste for the grand lifestyle, James made and lost multiple fortunes during his life. The "Hollywood" story ended as humbly as it began, for Lee Warren James died intestate, leaving a very modest probate estate of about $650 for each of his grandchildren.

CHAPTER THREE

THE J. BRADFORD COOLIDGE ERA

1938-1965

On Valentine's Day in 1886, Joseph Bradford Coolidge was born in the Boston suburb of Holliston, Massachusetts, the son of Edgar and Helen (Murphy) Coolidge. Brad Coolidge was a distant relative of President Calvin Coolidge. The histories and genealogies of the Coolidge families suggest that during the 1800s, the Coolidge families were centered in the Boston area, and most were educated at some of the top schools in the Northeast. Brad Coolidge spent his entire academic life in Boston, Massachusetts. He graduated with honors from the prestigious Boston Latin High School in 1904, earning a gold medal for Latin scholarship in the process. He then enrolled at Harvard College where he studied the classics and graduated with a Bachelor of Arts.

Dayton Latin School was located on Robert Boulevard which ran along the Miami River near the west side of downtown Dayton

Brad Coolidge came to Dayton and became the first Headmaster of Dayton Latin School, a private school designed to prepare students for admission and performance at the nation's top colleges and universities. Sometimes called "the Boulders" for its initial location in north Dayton View, the Dayton Latin School was later moved to 220 North Robert Boulevard, near the west side of downtown Dayton. Brad Coolidge taught at Dayton Latin School from the fall of 1907 until the spring of 1909. He must have made an impressive impact on the Dayton community, for his leadership of Dayton Latin School was noted in Drury's *History of City of Dayton and Montgomery County Ohio* published in 1909 — published after Brad Coolidge had already gone back to Boston to attend Harvard Law School.

Brad Coolidge retained his personal law school notes from his years at Harvard Law School. They have been bound in eight red leather volumes and are a special part of the Firm's archives. These notebooks provide a wonderful insight into Coolidge's life as a law student in the 1910 era. Each book contains his name, his address in Cambridge, the name of the course, the name of the professor, and often his seat number in class. (At this time, students at Harvard had assigned seats for each of their courses.)

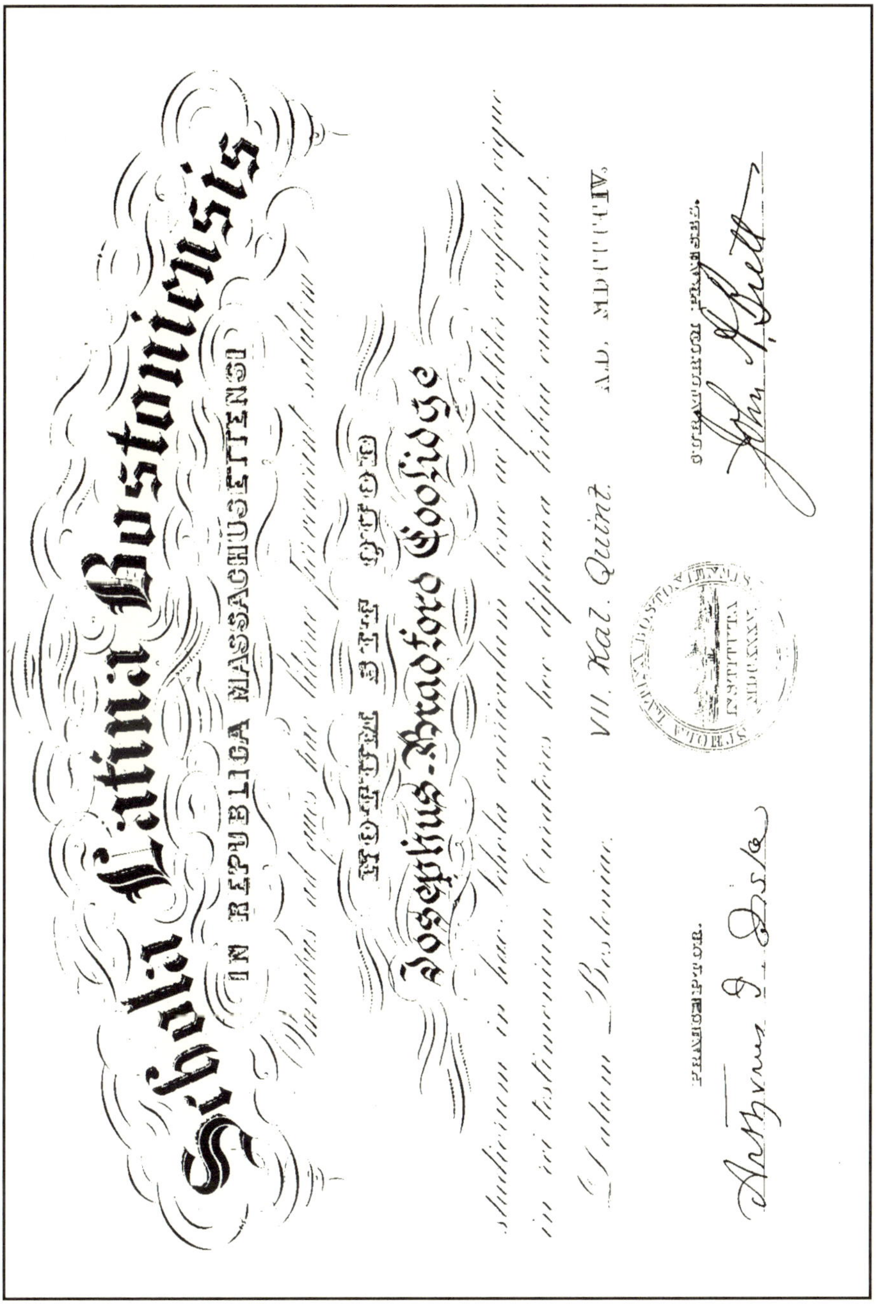
Schola Latina Bostoniensis
IN REPUBLICA MASSACHUSETTENSI
Josephus Bradford Coolidge
VII. Kal. Quint.

His law school notes are especially interesting because they mention his professors who were some of the most renowned legal scholars in their respective disciplines. For example, one of Coolidge's red notebooks is for his 1910-1911 Property II class from "Professor Gray". Professor Gray is John Chipman Gray (1839-1915) who is revered as the real property scholar who authored the famous treatise on the Rule Against Perpetuities and founded the Boston law firm of Ropes & Gray. The notes in the front of the book are as follows:

J. Bradford Coolidge 2L
10 Hilliard Street
Cambridge
Property II — Professor Gray 1910-1911

Each page of these notebooks is divided into two areas by a vertical blue line, one about twice the size of the other. On the larger side of each page, it appears that Coolidge used black ink to brief assigned cases in advance of class. He then used red ink to write his class notes and observations by the professor. His Property II class notes for Professor Gray are especially enlightening because Coolidge often inserted his own diagrams to illustrate the real estate parcels involved in the case. For example, one of the cases in his notebook is *Hall v. Eaton*, 139 Mass. 217, 29 N.E. 660 (Sup. Jud. Ct. Mass 1885), a property line dispute case in which the Supreme Judicial Court of Massachusetts ruled that the intent of the parties was best expressed in the language in the deed which recited that the new lot split line was to be "at right angles to Dix Street." The plaintiffs had proffered a drawing purporting to show that the lot split line should be at an obtuse angle so that it would be parallel to Wachusett Street. The opinion contained the following diagram:

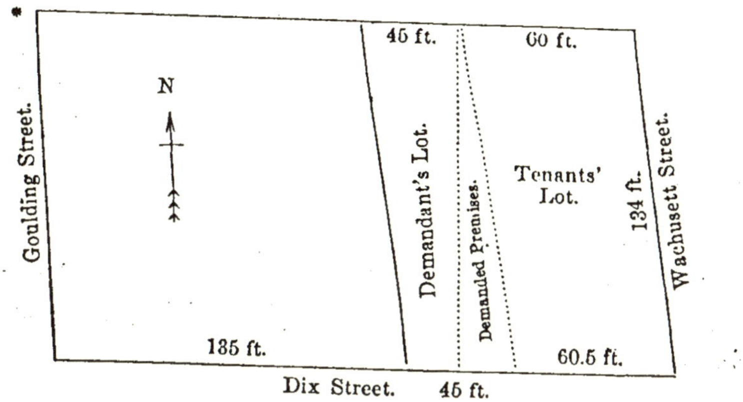

In his notebook, Coolidge drew his own survey of the property in dispute, and noted that the court held that the "right angle" language in the deed "best shows grantor's intent — Court of opinion that making the 3rd line at rt L's with Dix St showed that his shape was what was present in minds of parties."

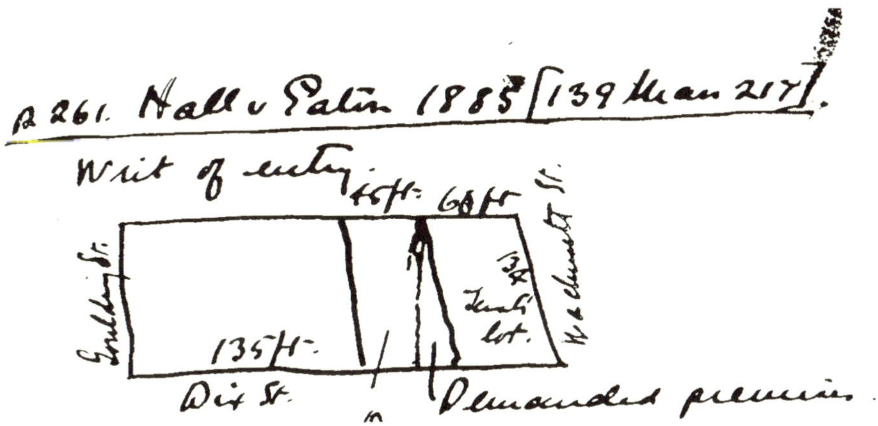

All of Brad Coolidge's notebooks are very meticulous and reflect not only his mastery of the law but also his discipline as a student. That attention to accuracy and detail was the hallmark of his practice throughout his entire career. Some of the other law school notebooks of Coolidge are for the following courses:

J. Bradford Coolidge 2L Seat 250
10 Hilliard Street
Cambridge

Evidence -- Dean Thayer 1910-11

* * *

J. Bradford Coolidge 2L Seat 107
10 Hilliard Street
Cambridge

Equity II-- Professor Pound 1910-11

Professor Pound was Roscoe Pound (1870-1964), the esteemed and prolific author and legal scholar who served at Harvard Law School from 1910 to 1937 as a professor of law. He also served as Dean of the Harvard Law School from 1916 to 1936.

J. Bradford Coolidge 2L
10 Hilliard Street
Cambridge

Sales -- Professor Williston 1910-11

Samuel Williston (1861-1963) served as a professor of law at Harvard Law School from 1890 to 1938. His treatise, *Williston on Contracts*, has been a benchmark of legal scholarship since its first publication. He also drafted the Uniform Sales Act, the predecessor to the Uniform Commercial Code.

On June 29, 1911, Brad Coolidge married Elizabeth ("Betty") Peirce, the daughter of J. Elliot Peirce and Fannie Harsh of Dayton. The Peirces owned and operated the Algonquin Hotel at the southwest corner of Third and Ludlow Streets. (This hotel building would be subsequently known over the years as the Gibbons Hotel, the Daytonian, and, more recently, the Doubletree Hotel.) The wedding took place on the lawn at the stately Peirce family home at the northeast corner of Five Oaks and Old Orchard Avenue in Dayton View. The bridal party was announced by the Heidelberg Orchestra. The ceremony was conducted by Reverend Maurice Wilson, pastor of the First Presbyterian Church. After the wedding, the bride and groom honeymooned in Nova Scotia before they returned to Boston so that he could complete his last year of law school.

From that marriage, there were two daughters: Mary Coolidge and Dorothy Coolidge. Mary Coolidge married Robert Oelman who later served as Chairman of NCR Corporation during the late 1960s and early 1970s. Dorothy Coolidge married Robert Woodward.

Brad Coolidge was graduated from Harvard Law School in 1912. When he took the Ohio bar examination that summer he was awarded the highest passing mark. He began the practice of law in Dayton in 1912 as an Assistant City Attorney for the City of Dayton. By 1913 he was associated with Lee Warren James and the Firm in its fifth floor suite in the U.B. Building.

In May 1916 Coolidge became a principal in the Firm with Lee Warren James, a relationship that would continue until 1937. It was also in the U.B. Building that Brad Coolidge met Loren M. Berry and started a relationship that would continue throughout the lives of both. After Lee Warren James left the Firm and Coolidge moved the Firm to the Callahan Building, Peirce Wood and William J. Bradley joined the practice. Bill Bradley was born on October 12, 1913, and joined the Firm in 1937 after graduating from the University of Dayton and University of Cincinnati Law School.

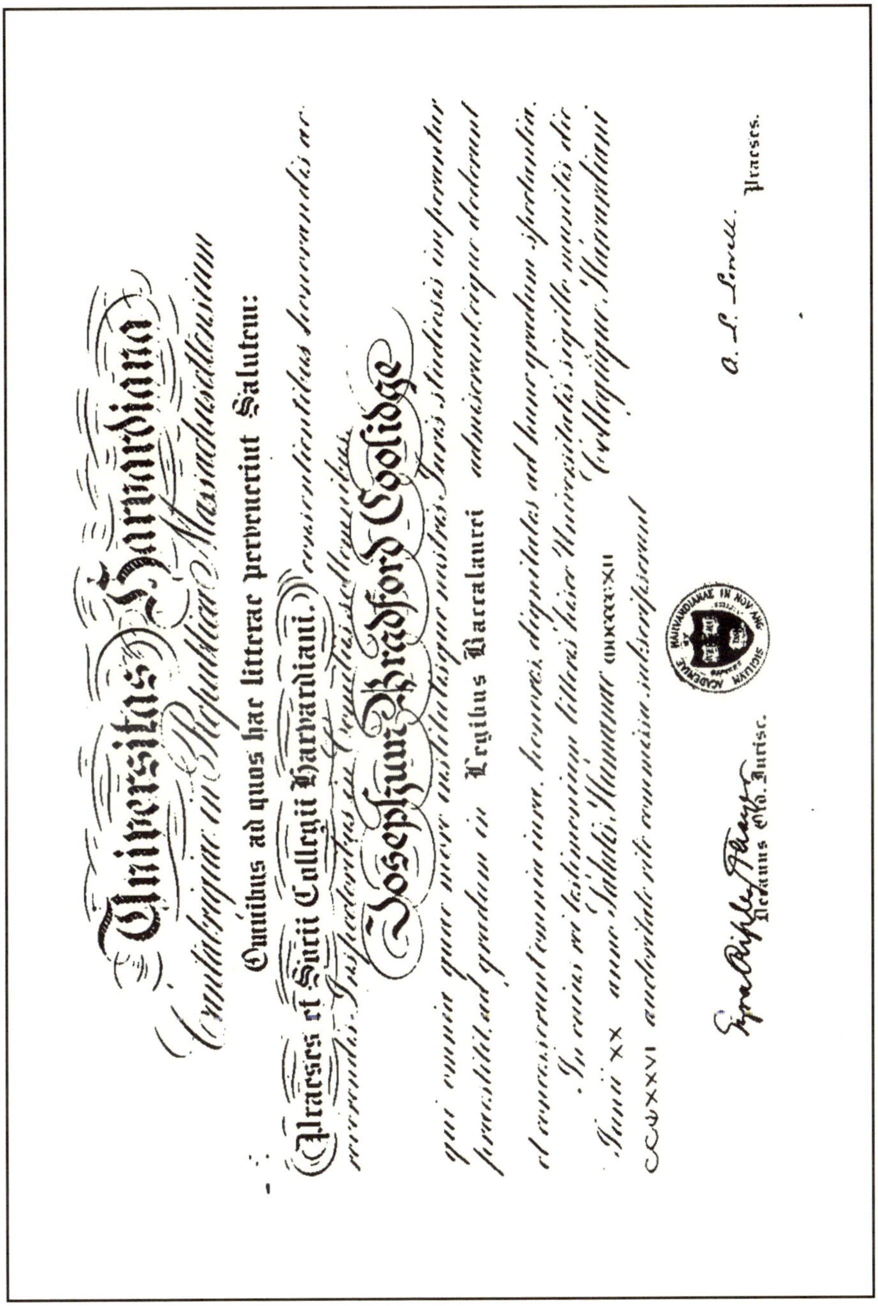
Universitas Harvardiana

Cantabrigiae in Republica Massachusettensium

Omnibus ad quos hae litterae pervenerint Salutem:

Praeses et Socii Collegii Harvardiani, consentientibus honorandis ac reverendis Inspectoribus in Comitiis sollemnibus

Josephum Bradford Coolidge

qui omnia quae more institutisque nostris Juris studiosis imperantur praestitit, ad gradum in Legibus Baccalaurei admiserunt, eique dederunt et concesserunt omnia iura, honores, dignitates ad hunc gradum spectantia.

In cuius rei testimonium litteris hisce Universitatis sigillo munitis die Junii XX anno Salutis Humanae MDCCCCXII Collegiique Harvardiani CCLXXVI auctoritate rite commissa subscripserunt

Ezra Ripley Thayer
Decanus Ord. Jurisc.

A. L. Lowell.
Praeses.

JOSEPH BRADFORD COOLIDGE
PHILIP R. BECKER
WILLIAM J. BRADLEY
PEIRCE WOOD

Coolidge & Becker

Law Offices—Twelfth Floor Callahan Bldg.
Tels. ADams 8177-8178

Peirce Wood was born on November 16, 1914 in Columbus, Ohio. The Wood family had an exceptional background in education and government service. His grandfather, Thomas J. Wood attended the United States Military Academy at West Point. During the Civil War he served as Commander of the Army of Ohio and was in virtually every battle within Sherman's March to the Sea. After his military career, Major General Thomas J. Wood lived in Dayton until his death in 1906. He was buried at West Point.

Pete Wood's father was George Henry Wood who was graduated from Yale University and then University of Cincinnati Law School. He too spent the major portion of his career in military service, rising to the position of Adjutant-General of Ohio and leading a division of the Ohio National Guard, known as the "Buckeye Division" in World War I in France and Belgium. On June 29, 1910, George Henry Wood married Virginia Peirce, daughter of J. Elliot and Fannie Harsh Peirce and sister of the wife of Brad Coolidge. They had two children, Thomas J. Wood, III, commonly known as T. J., and Peirce Wood, commonly known as Pete.

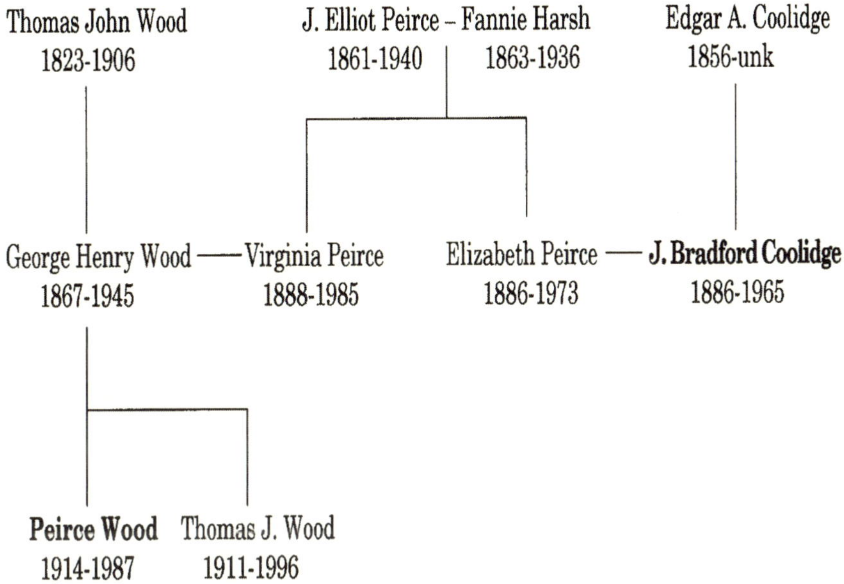

T. J. Wood and Pete Wood were both graduated from Oakwood High School and then Williams College in Williamstown, Massachusetts. After that, T. J. Wood first went to Ohio State for a master's degree and, then he and Pete Wood both attended Harvard University. T. J. Wood graduated with a Ph.D. in government and political science, and Pete Wood with a Bachelor of Laws degree.

T. J. Wood stayed in academia, teaching first at Oakwood High School and then for a number of years at Williams College, where he also served as the Director of Admissions from 1938 to 1947. T. J. Wood finally tired of the harsh winters in northwest Massachusetts and headed south to Florida, where he was appointed Professor of Government at the University of Miami in Coral Gables. He taught there until his death in 1996.

Meanwhile, after graduating from Harvard Law School, Pete Wood returned to Dayton and began working for his uncle, Brad Coolidge at the Firm. Despite the family connection, no one who knew either Brad Coolidge or Pete Wood would think for a minute that Coolidge would hire a relative simply because he was a relative or that Wood would ever accept a job for which he was not eminently qualified.

Not long after Bill Bradley and Pete Wood joined the Firm, World War II broke out, first in Europe, later in the Pacific. On the day after the attack on Pearl Harbor on December 7, 1941, Pete Wood rushed out and sent telegrams to the Secretary of Navy and to J. Edgar Hoover, the Director of the Federal Bureau of Investigation with the following message:

WESTERN UNION

J. Edgar Hoover
Federal Bureau of Investigation
Washington, D.C.

I am a graduate of Williams College and Harvard Law School. • I want to join your organization in service of my country. •

Peirce Wood

December 8, 1941

J. Edgar Hoover immediately accepted his proposal and Pete Wood worked for the FBI as a Special Agent during World War II, often assigned to do undercover surveillance of persons suspected of acting against the United States.

The war also interrupted the career of Bill Bradley. In early 1941, Bill Bradley left the Firm to join the FBI and reportedly was sent as an undercover agent to Rio de Janeiro where he served throughout World War II as an attaché with the American Embassy. There, he met and married the daughter of an American lawyer who had a lucrative law practice in Rio. Bradley stayed in Rio after the war and worked in his father-in-law's firm.

In 1945, after the war, Wood returned to Dayton and reconsidered his future and whether he even wanted to practice law. Over a drink at the Biltmore Hotel, Hugh Wall, who had joined Coolidge at the Firm in 1941, urged him to pursue private practice with him and Brad Coolidge. Wood decided to do that and started a long and legendary career.

It was the departure of Bill Bradley from the Firm in early 1941 that created the opening for Hugh E. Wall, Jr., to join the Firm. Hugh E. Wall, Jr., was born on April 14, 1912, the son of Hugh E. Wall, Sr., an accountant early with the National Cash Register Co. and later the head of the largest independent CPA firm in Dayton. Hugh E. Wall, Jr., graduated from Chaminade High School in 1929, the University of Dayton (A.B.) in 1933, and the University of Notre Dame (LL.B.) in 1936. On September 22, 1938, he married Clare Aull who was born on April 25, 1914.

After graduation from Notre Dame, Hugh Wall, Jr., of course, had to take the Ohio bar exam in Columbus. To get there, he rode with Bob Crew in Bob's new 1936 Ford convertible. Bob Crew was a boyhood friend who had graduated from Oakwood High School in 1929, the same year that Hugh Wall had graduated from Chaminade High School.

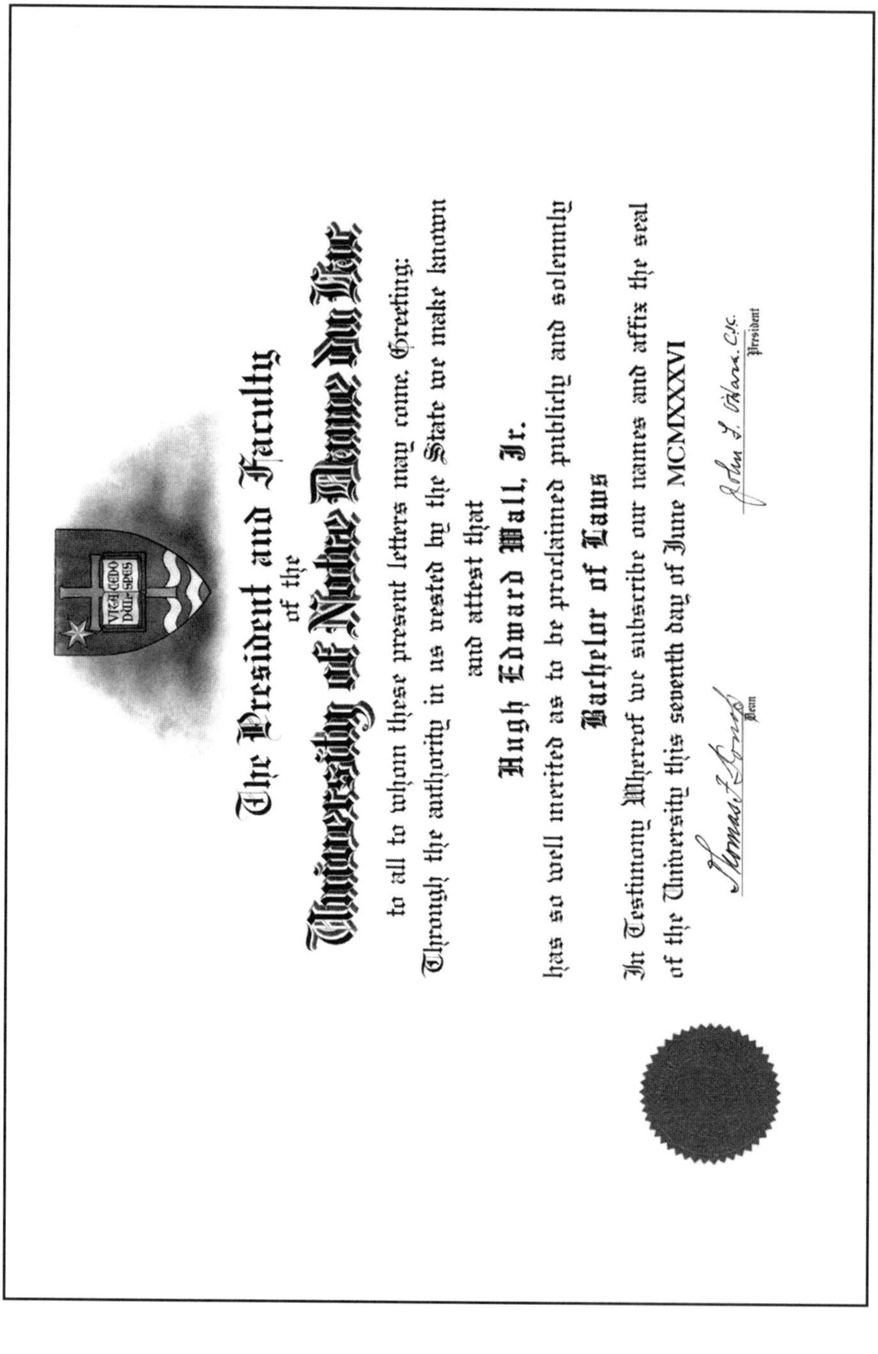

The President and Faculty
of the
University of Notre Dame du Lac
to all to whom these present letters may come, Greeting:
Through the authority in us vested by the State we make known
and attest that
Hugh Edward Wall, Jr.
has so well merited as to be proclaimed publicly and solemnly
Bachelor of Laws
In Testimony Whereof we subscribe our names and affix the seal
of the University this seventh day of June MCMXXXVI

Dean

President

Hugh E. Wall, Jr.
1912-2001
1936 Graduation photograph
Notre Dame Law School

In 1936, Bob Crew had just graduated from Northwestern Law School. So they drove over to Columbus, with the top down, excited and anxious about their upcoming ordeal. When they arrived in Columbus, all of the hotels were taken because of a big convention going on in Columbus. Eventually, Wall found them sleeping rooms at the Knights of Columbus hall, with the restrooms down the hall. Luckily, both were well prepared and, despite the rather wild beginning, easily passed the bar exam and were admitted to practice.

Hugh Wall went to Washington, D.C., as an associate with Alvis & Grainey, a small law firm that concentrated exclusively on federal tax cases. In those days all cases that were not resolved in the auditing with a revenue agent were referred to the Appellate Division, which sat only in Washington, D.C. Consequently, unresolved tax cases from all over the country were referred to Washington law firms, and tax work was plentiful and lucrative.

In the early 1940's, the Internal Revenue Service started a decentralized plan which caused Hugh Wall to believe that tax work would subside in Washington and build up in the various regional IRS districts. He thought it was the right time to return to Dayton and continue his tax practice there. The tax experience in Washington made him attractive to a number of Dayton law firms. Hugh Wall sought advice from his boyhood hero, Gene Mayl. (Gene Mayl was a local Dayton legend because he had played with the great George Gipp under Knute Rockne at Notre Dame. After football, Gene Mayl returned to Dayton to practice law.) Gene Mayl helped Hugh Wall sift through the offers from Dayton law firms, often telling him, "That's pretty good, Hugh, but I don't think you'd be happy there." When he got to the offer from Brad Coolidge, Gene Mayl said, "Now, that's the one to take." Hugh Wall, Jr., took the offer, joining Brad Coolidge on July 1, 1941.

Gunckel & Rowe
Federal Reporter-1st Series
Volumes 1-3
1880

Gunckel & Strong
Attorneys at Law
Copy Letter Books
Firm Correspondence
1853-1863

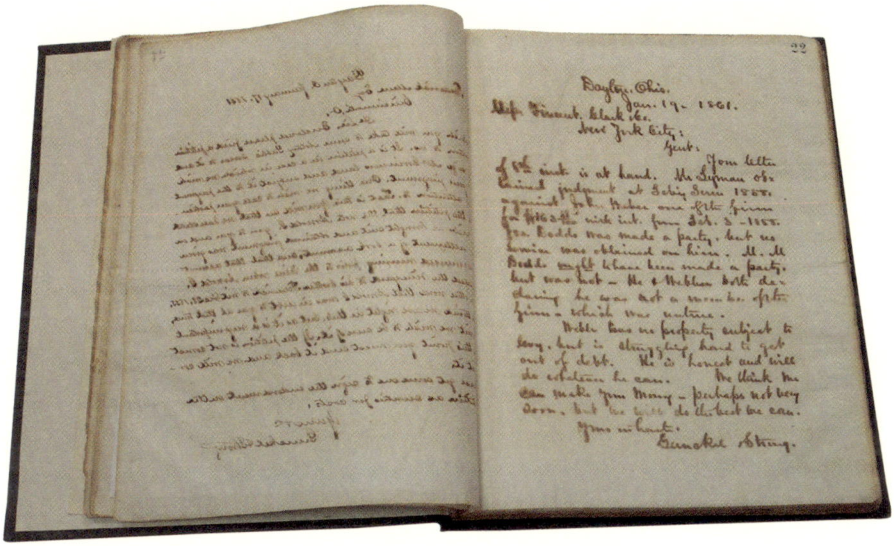

Gunckel & Strong
Attorneys at Law
Copy Letter Book
Letter to Viscount Clark Co.
New York City
January 19, 1861

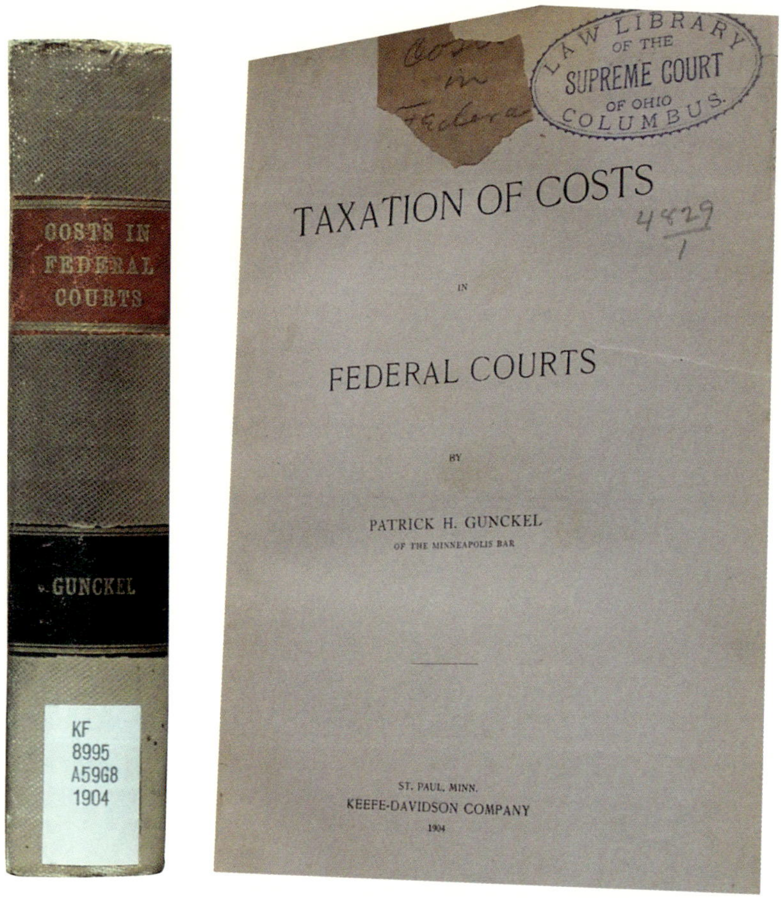

Patrick H. Gunckel,
Author
Taxation of Costs in Federal Courts
1904
Published by Keefe-Davidson Company
St. Paul, Minnesota
(Courtesy Law Library of Ohio Supreme Court)

Edward L. Rowe, Esq.
Federal Reporter-1st Series
Volumes 110, 121
1901, 1903

Joseph Bradford Coolidge
Class Notes
Harvard Law School
1910-1911

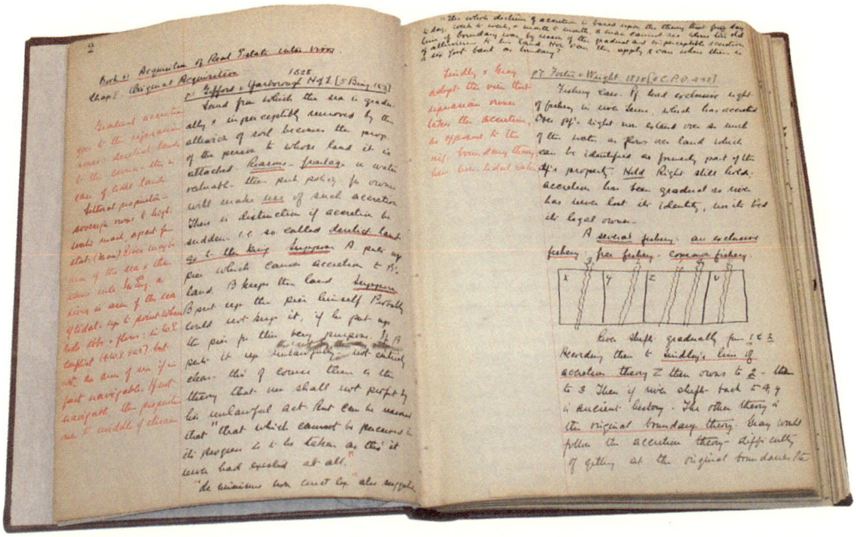

Joseph Bradford Coolidge
Foster v. Wright, 4 C.P.D. 438 (1878)
English Common Pleas Division
Property Class Notes
Harvard Law School
October 3, 1910

Lee Warren James
Federal Reporter-1st Series
Volumes 108-109, 112-113
1901-1902

When Hugh Wall, Jr., arrived in 1941, the Firm was still using the letter copying press that Gunckel & Strong had purchased on March 8, 1853, when the Firm first opened for business. For over ninety years the letter copying press was the only method of retaining file copies of letters sent out. It was still a messy and time-consuming process. Of course, by then the secretaries used typewriters for the originals and at the end of each day, they would go through the same copying process described earlier in this book. The secretaries hated it. Finally, the production shifts caused by World War II eliminated all sources for the letter press copying books. Coolidge gave up and said "We'd better change our system." The Firm upgraded to carbon paper for which the secretaries were very thankful, at least until the next upgrade in letter copying became available.

In 1949, James E. Rambo joined the Firm as an associate. He was born on July 26, 1924, graduating from Oakwood High School in 1941. He too was swept into World War II, serving for three years in the Army Corps of Engineers. After the war, he was educated at Ohio University and the University of Cincinnati School of Law before being admitted to the Ohio bar in 1949. Jim Rambo worked at the Firm under Brad Coolidge for five years and then served as an Assistant United States Attorney in Dayton for another three years. With that experience, Jim Rambo joined NCR's Law Department, leading to a very distinguished career as General Counsel of NCR from 1965 until 1984.

Another Firm lawyer who has been long remembered was Edgar J. Graef, Jr., popularly known as Eddy Graef. He was born on February 28, 1926, and grew up in Oakwood. While attending high school, he starred as a basketball player and golfer. Getting out of high school at the peak of World War II, he joined the Navy and served for two years. Upon his return, he first attended and graduated from Williams

College and then attended and graduated from Harvard Law School. Upon being admitted to practice law in 1952, Eddy Graef joined the Firm. By 1955, the Firm's listing in Martindale-Hubbell was as follows:

General Practice Corporation, Probate, Insurance, Tax and Labor Law	**COOLIDGE, WALL AND WOOD** 12TH FLOOR, CALLAHAN BUILDING **DAYTON 2, OHIO**	*Telephone: ADams 8177*

MEMBERS OF FIRM

Joseph Bradford Coolidge, born Holliston, Massachusetts, February 14, 1886; admitted to bar, 1912, Ohio. Preparatory education, Boston Latin School, 1904 and Harvard College (A.B., 1908); legal education, Harvard Law School (LL.B., 1912). *Member:* Lawyers Club; Dayton, The Ohio State and American Bar Associations.

Hugh E. Wall, Jr., born Dayton, Ohio, April 14, 1912; admitted to bar, 1936, Ohio. Preparatory education, Chaminade and University of Dayton (A.B., 1933); legal education, Notre Dame Law School (LL.B., 1936). *Member:* Lawyers Club; Barristers Club (President, 1943); Dayton, The Ohio State (Member, Tax Committee, 1953-1955) and American (Member, Partnership Section of Tax Committee, 1952—) Bar Associations.

Peirce Wood, born Columbus, Ohio, November 16, 1914; admitted to bar, 1939, Ohio. Preparatory education, Williams College (A.B., 1936); legal education, Harvard Law School (LL.B., 1939). *Fraternity:* Phi Beta Kappa. *Member:* Lawyers Club; Dayton, The Ohio State and American Bar Associations.

ASSOCIATE

Edgar J. Graef, Jr., born Dayton, Ohio, February 28, 1926; admitted to bar, 1953, Ohio. Preparatory education, Williams College (A.B., 1949); legal education, Harvard University (LL.B., 1952). *Member:* Dayton Bar Association. [U. S, Navy, 1944-1946]

Eddy Graef was developing a good practice when on April 2, 1963, he walked out of the office at the end of the day, collapsed on the sidewalk on Main Street, and died at the age of 37. It was a shocking loss to his family and to the Firm. He is interred at the Dayton Memorial Park Cemetery.

At about this time, Brad Coolidge hired Robert B. Matusoff, a recent graduate of the University of Michigan (B.A., 1951) and Harvard Law School (LL.B., *cum laude* 1954). Bob Matusoff was born March 3, 1930, the son of Lou and Freda Matusoff and graduated from Dayton's Fairview High School in 1947. After law school, Bob work at House,

Robert B. Matusoff

Grossman, Vorhaus & Hemley at 521 Fifth Avenue in New York, before starting at the Firm on May 1, 1956.

His hiring at Coolidge might well have seemed notable at the time because Bob Matusoff became the first Jewish lawyer in the Firm. Several facts augured in his favor. The fact that Bob Matusoff had graduated from Harvard gave him a foot in the door with Brad Coolidge who had two Harvard degrees of his own. In addition, Hugh Wall, Jr., had been friends with Lou Matusoff since they were both kids folding pants at the old Metropolitan Department Store then located at 4th and Ludlow in the building now occupied by Wilkies Bookstore and the Reynolds + Reynolds Company. Hugh Wall and Lou Matusoff continued their friendship as adults while both were active in the United Fellowship of Christians and Jews.

Bob Matusoff discounted any theory that Hugh Wall had influenced Brad Coolidge to hire him — or anyone else. "Brad Coolidge did what Brad Coolidge wanted to do." The most important factors were that Brad Coolidge fundamentally liked Bob Matusoff, thought he would enhance the Firm's business, and invited him to join the Firm. Just as Coolidge thought, Bob Matusoff developed quickly as a lawyer, both in working with clients and with his corporate and securities law expertise. That talent and expertise would serve him well and would serve the Firm well during his tenure at the Firm.

Robert B. Womsley also joined the Firm in the late 1950s. Born on February 6, 1933, in Wheeling, West Virginia, Bob Womsley attended Cranbrook School in Birmingham, Michigan, and moved to Dayton when his parents, Robert and Nellie Womsley, moved to Dayton and his father became the head of the Trust Department at Winters Bank. Bob Womsley was graduated from Brown University (B.A., 1955) and the University of Cincinnati (LL.B., 1958). Originally

Robert B. Womsley

intending to go into the Air Force, Womsley began working at the Firm on a part-time basis. When the Air Force reduced its forces and career opportunities. Coolidge asked him, "Well, are you having fun here, and do you want to stay here?" With that two sentence interview, Bob Womsley passed muster and joined the Firm to begin a legal career which has now extended over forty years.

Following closely behind Bob Womsley in joining the Firm was John C. Lombard, who arrived at the Firm in 1964. His family had deep New England roots. Lombard was born in Worcester, Massachusetts, on August 19, 1927. His family had owned and operated Riggs & Lombard, a manufacturer of textile finishing machinery, enabling him to attend and graduate from both Phillips Exeter Academy (1945) and Harvard University (1950). Initially, he worked for The Wyman & Gordon Co., a drop-forging plant located in Worcester. While working, he attended Boston College Law School. He was admitted to the Massachusetts bar in 1959 and continued to work for The Wyman & Gordon Co. for four more years.

When John Lombard decided to enter into private practice, he had a flicker of interest in Ohio, initially sparked by his relationship to Dayton's Kettering family. Lombard's brother, Dick Lombard, was married to Jane Kettering, the daughter of Gene and Virginia Kettering. With that family relationship, working for Brad Coolidge was a natural opportunity. Given the experiences of his own relocation from Boston to Ohio, Brad Coolidge had some apprehension about bringing a New Englander to the Ohio frontier, but, Brad Coolidge liked John Lombard, and, in turn, John Lombard liked Brad Coolidge, liked the Firm, and liked the Dayton community. With that invitation, John Lombard brought his New England accent with him to Ohio.

John C. Lombard

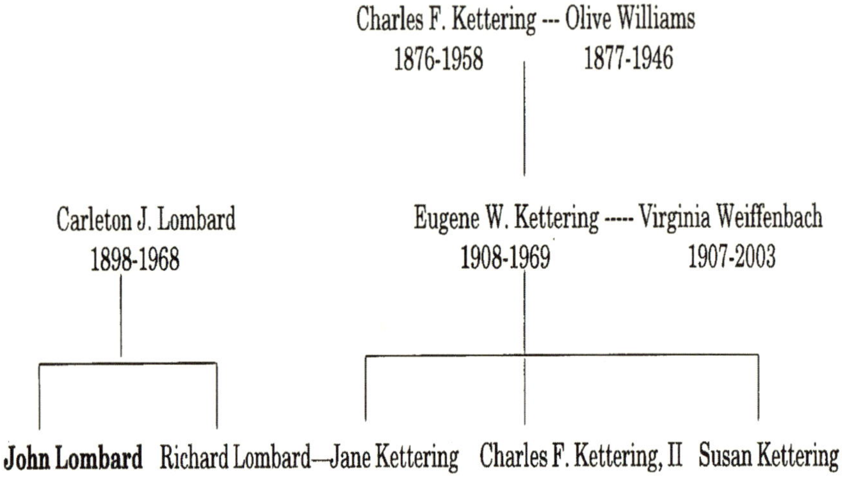

While Brad Coolidge always had an aura of aristocracy about him, it was a sense of aristocracy from which Pete Wood never suffered. In an incident which reflects both the changing times and Brad Coolidge's sense of style and worldview, Pete Wood on an outing with Brad Coolidge, once proudly displayed a large collection of credit cards in an accordion wallet – at a time when credit cards were first coming into use. Looking down on Wood with some disdain, Brad Coolidge dismissed the exhibition with the terse comment that "a man of his stature should have just a line of credit or at least be known in his community."

Peirce Wood
1914-1987

The aristocratic formality of Brad Coolidge stood in stark contrast to the almost-eccentric appearance of Pete Wood, for Wood typically had a burr hair cut which went nicely with his white socks and bow tie — except during his courtroom work when Wood would wear his Harvard tie in a Windsor knot on the last day of trial.

In his legal practice, however, Pete Wood's superiority was never doubted. He was an excellent courtroom lawyer who was as quick on his feet as anyone in the Dayton legal community. With his classic educational background, he could quote Latin phrases, Shakespeare, and other great authors as a part of his natural conversation. More than one associate at the Firm was told by Wood to meet him "prima luce" the next day so that they could tackle a job together. He did so with a natural air of such confidence that it sometimes appeared to others as an intellectual chip on his shoulder.

Pete Wood concentrated primarily on zoning and condemnation cases, usually presenting his cases at the appropriate zoning board, plan board, city council or panel of township trustees. Many of the Firm lawyers got their early experience working with Pete Wood on these zoning and appropriation cases. Bob Matusoff spent part of his early years helping Pete Wood on a number of appropriation cases, including those in which they represented many of the landowners ceding right of way for the initial construction of I-75 through Dayton. At one point, Pete Wood and Bob Matusoff were walking the property of a mobile home park near Woody's Market in West Carrollton, Ohio, in order to measure their claims. When it got to trial, Pete Wood put Bob Matusoff on the stand and qualified him as an expert to get those measurements into evidence for the jury to consider.

One of Pete Wood's favorite cases was the protracted zoning litigation regarding what was then known as

Normandy Farms, a residual 400 acre tract that was originally attached to the Richard H. Grant family home (now transformed into the Normandy United Methodist Church) at the corner of Normandy Lane and Alex-Bell Road. Normandy Farms was located generally south of Alex-Bell Road and west of Normandy Lane in Washington Township, but it was an irregular parcel which at one point extended west all the way to McEwen Road.

The Grant family was challenging a zoning classification which zoned its property into minimum 80,000 square foot lots (almost two acres) for a single family residence. Pete Wood and Bob Womsley worked on this case together, often meeting together in the evening to socialize and strategize. In the current climate of routine Power Point presentations, their preparation of the exhibits for this case is both insightful and astounding. Using a large topographic map of the northwest quadrant of Washington Township, which had been prepared by Ralph Woolpert, they sawed a sheet of half inch thick plywood into a forty inch square.

Using one of those tools that are now infamously termed "box cutters," Pete Wood and Bob Womsley cut strips of thick cardboard to match the topographic lines of the flat map and built up, layer by layer, a three dimensional map of the terrain of Normandy Farm as it lay within the northwest quadrant of Washington Township, showing the high ridge lines and the deep ravines along Holes Creek in ten foot increments from a 750 foot elevation to a 1050 foot elevation. Then they painted the map, keying the colors to the different zoning classifications.

In order to use the map as an exhibit in both the administrative hearings and the judicial trials, Pete Wood put Bob Womsley under oath to educe the preparation of the map to make it admissible. The Minutes of the Washington Township Zoning Board Public Hearing on March 6, 1961, record its use:

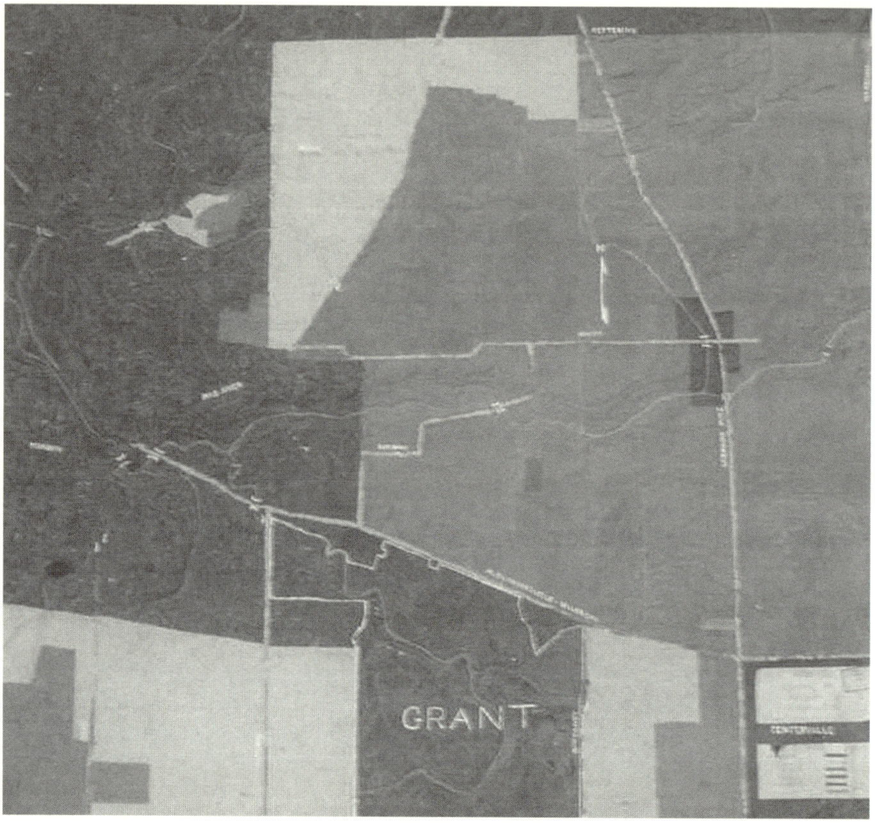

Normandy Farms Zoning Litigation

The 1961 three dimensional contour map constructed in ten layers of cardboard cut by a "boxcutters" tool to show the changing elevation in ten foot increments.

In concluding his presentation Mr. Wood, with the assistance of Mr. Womsley, showed the Board and those present an elaborate 3-dimensional contour map of the Grant property and brought forth points of interest to all concerned.

No less energy or precision went into the creation of legal documents. The lengthy trial and appellate briefs in this case show the extraordinary intellectual edge Pete employed in constructing his arguments:

- The Court's confusion no doubt stemmed from the Germanically inverted sentence structure found in Section 519.02.

- To attempt to derive the fair market value of plaintiff's 400 acres from the price paid for nearby two acre tracts is comparable to using the store price of kitchen matches to arrive at the value of standing timber.

- Only battle-scarred veterans of the Washington Township zoning wars could be expected to understand and remember the patchwork of zoning that the township has put together in the guise of promoting public health, safety and morals. Indeed, the map showing the actual zoning status of the developed plats in Washington Township is reminiscent of a map of the Holy Roman Empire in the 17th and 18th centuries.

- If the number of fires (or measles, murder or morals cases) is to be controlled by limiting through its two acre zoning the number of people who will live on the Grant farm, then every part of the township should be zoned similarly. It is equally important to control fires (and measles, murder and morals cases) in the areas now zoned for one acre, three-quarters of an acre and half-acre lots.

- The township seeks to continue to enforce the two acre zoning, although only thirteen per cent of its citizens originally favored its adoption as shown by the postcard poll taken by the "Committee of 500" and although only ten per cent favor it today. The township insists that regardless of personal desires, the ninety per cent must listen to Beethoven, look at Rembrandt and read Keats.

The Grant farm litigation extended for several years (*State of Ohio ex rel. Grant v. Kiefaber,* 171 Ohio St 326 (1960); *In Re Appeal of Grant*, 1 Ohio App. 2d 84, (2nd App District 1963)). During the retrial following the most recent appellate decision, Judge Carl D. Kessler had ruled in favor of the Grant family interests in a number of evidentiary matters. In a status report memorandum to Richard Grant, Pete Wood explored the concept of settlement. Recognizing that if the judge ruled that two acre zoning was unconstitutional, there might be dire consequences to the Township beyond his property, Pete Wood cautioned him to consider some type of compromise:

> From your standpoint, the acceptance of something less than a complete victory also might be advisable. Presumably you will live in the township for many more years. You will not want to be remembered as the Joshua who brought the walls of Jericho tumbling down.
>
> Samuel Butler in a speech to the Rump Parliament said: "It hath been said that an unjust peace is to be preferred before a just war."

Eventually, a resolution was reached, terminating the litigation and effectively terminating the two acre minimum zoning requirement for Normandy Farms, in exchange for which, Washington Township was deeded certain parkland along Holes Creek (now known as Grant Park).

Pete Wood lived at 26 Patterson Road in Oakwood and shared a driveway with John Remick. In addition, Wood and Remick had a common professional interest because Remick was an appraiser and property manager, whose work fit in well with Wood's zoning and condemnation practice. Both were hard workers and were almost in competition with each other in their commitment to their respective professional practices. Each recalls waking up early in the morning – or in the middle of the night – to see if the other one was working. John Remick would often see Pete Wood sitting in his kitchen at 2:00 a.m. eating Graham crackers and drinking an occasional beer while pounding away on his old Royal manual typewriter.

In the same way, Pete Wood pounded away on all his cases. Often he was pursuing a course of action which was unpopular, whether it was a proposed commercial rezoning opposed by local residents or whether it was Joseph Thal and Arthur Beerman successfully opposing the proposed walkway across Ludlow which would have connected the Rike's Department Store to its parking garage. The public hearings on these cases often produced huge crowds who were vehemently opposed to the action he was promoting. Pete Wood and his clients were often vastly outnumbered, yet, he doggedly pled his case. It was his nature to represent an unpopular client or unpopular position and to pursue it without regard to his critics. Throughout his career, Pete Wood loved the challenge – loved being the rebel with a cause.

Coolidge's legal career spanned more than fifty years. Throughout his career and throughout his life — and in many ways the two intertwined — Brad Coolidge exemplified the image of a highly intellectual, highly sophisticated professional who set extremely high standards for himself and expected extremely high performance from those who worked for him. At the peak of his practice, Joseph Bradford Coolidge was the pre-eminent business lawyer in Dayton. He was a member of the board of directors for Winters National Bank & Trust Co., Reynolds + Reynolds Company, Huffman Manufacturing Company, The Kettering Foundation, the Gallaher Drug Co. and Oakwood Railway Co. In addition, Coolidge served as primary counsel to Loren M. Berry in the Yellow Pages directory business from 1921 until Coolidge's death in 1965.

Coolidge's need to control all aspects of his legal practice was evidenced by the Firm's structure as a sole proprietorship. Legally, his practice would be described as

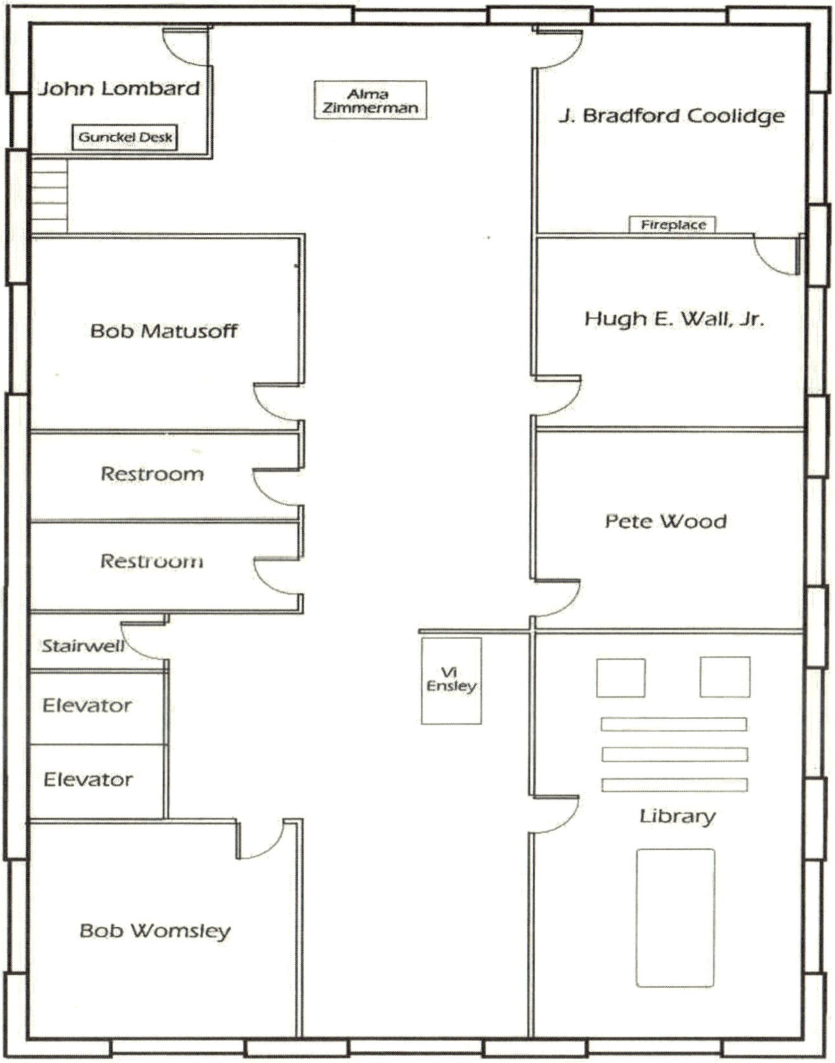

This is the Firm twelfth floor plan in the Callahan / Gem Savings Building. Because of office movements during this period this is a representative configuration.

"J. Bradford Coolidge doing business as 'Coolidge, Wall & Wood.'" Hugh E. Wall, Jr. and Peirce Wood were actually employees of Brad Coolidge throughout their early careers and rise to prominence in the Dayton legal community. It is a tribute to Coolidge's stature and a tribute to Pete Wood's and Hugh Wall's enduring patience and foresight that they accepted this arrangement. Both of them would have had numerous opportunities over the years to associate themselves with other good lawyers or to start their own firms, but, in the long run, their strategy was best, for in electing to stay with Coolidge, they had the opportunity to succeed to his practice upon his departure.

No one who worked for Brad Coolidge (including Hugh Wall who worked for him for twenty five years) had any doubt as to whose law firm it was. It was Brad Coolidge's law firm. To punctuate his authority and control, Coolidge always opened all of the mail, no matter to whom it was addressed. Even electricity served as a lightning rod of control. Brad Coolidge believed that as long as there was daylight, you did not need electric lights. Ron Pretekin often had his library research interrupted by Coolidge walking into the library to shut off the lights. Of course, in fairness to Coolidge, the library on the twelfth floor of the Gem Savings Building was on the corner of the building with two big windows on the South and one big window on the West. His policies were rigorous but not unfair.

Coolidge set high standards of performance for himself, and he demanded that everyone else meet those standards. Perfection in writing was the goal his legal associates respected most and feared most. As Hugh Wall, Jr. said of Brad Coolidge,

> I have never been exposed to anybody who had a more precise mind. He was a gold medal

> scholar at the Boston Latin School, and when he took the Ohio Bar, he was No. 1 - - he was brilliant! He was small of stature, very precise, highly critical, but he could take a paragraph and condense it into a short sentence better than anybody I ever knew. He could dictate a fifteen-page trust agreement without looking at any form or anything else. And he was a master of English grammar. If you drafted something and didn't have the adverb following the verb, it would come back with a blue pencil through it. He was a great teacher - tough to work for, but very fair. Great training! He had the respect of anybody who ever did work for him, because he was very precise.

Bob Womsley had similar experiences with Brad Coolidge. "What Coolidge could do with his blue pencil to a letter I wrote was something else. It was always very constructive, and he was always absolutely right." Coolidge's never-ending demand for being concise and grammatically correct was an enduring legacy – so much so that it evoked a special tribute from the Dayton Bar Association in its Memorial Resolution:

> He was a precise man, sparing in the use of words. His friends and foes alike paid heed when Brad Coolidge suggested that two pages of verbiage be condensed into a paragraph, that a paragraph be shortened into a sentence or that a sentence be eliminated entirely.

Coolidge was a schoolmaster and a task master. He enjoyed a rare combination of great intellectual skill and tremendous business acumen. At the same time, he suffered from the curse of expecting the same skills and insights from others. His high expectations, coupled with his low tolerance of mediocrity, produced a demanding perfectionist against whom it was difficult to measure up. By all outward appearances, he satisfied his own standards, as virtually everyone who had ever dealt with him would attest.

No one remembers Brad Coolidge in a casual way. Indeed, no one remembers Coolidge in anything but a coat and tie, and that coat and tie never came off any day during his career at the Firm. Bob Matusoff was the first to challenge this part of the Firm culture by taking off his jacket during the day. Brad Coolidge at one point even instructed Hugh Wall, "Fire that young man for not keeping his coat on." Bob Matusoff responded, "Mr. Coolidge, I will move from the twelfth floor to the eleventh floor if I can take my coat off." In the end Brad Coolidge relented and suffered Matusoff's transgression with only occasional reminders. Coolidge might have foreseen the day when the Firm, under his name, would have fifty lawyers; he could never have foreseen Casual Friday.

In what was an annual Christmas ritual, Brad Coolidge would gather all the Firm lawyers on Christmas Eve so that they could "split the pie" (a more elegant vision than squirrels dividing walnuts). Of course, since Brad Coolidge absolutely controlled the Firm, he could split the pie and hand out whatever bonuses he deemed appropriate. Before he made those distributions, he first opened a bottle of brandy, poured a glass for each lawyer, and proposed a toast to the success of the Firm and the success of everyone's family. Then he gave each a piece of the pie. The practice of pre-Christmas year-end bonuses continued even after Coolidge's death, later taking the form of the December 15th combined year-end salary and bonus, so that lawyers and staff could use it to celebrate their own Christmas.

Firm office procedures and technologies during the 1950s and early 1960s were still at the World War II level - - the letter copying press had been replaced by carbon paper and a 3M Thermo-Fax machine, but word processing was still more an individual creation than a production press run. During those days, the last wills and testaments were typically manually typed on a stationery store form that, when folded once, created two legal sized pages. This created four "connected" sides of paper on which to type the (single spaced) document; of course, that meant a secretary would have to retype all four pages if there was an error on the fourth page. Bob Womsley recalled with great admiration how well the secretarial staff typed: "God love those secretaries. They were very good."

It is now difficult to imagine the routine mess created by trying to erase the typing on an original and then erase the same mistake on the multiple carbons. When the Xerox machine finally came on the market in the late 1950s and early 1960s, Bob Matusoff made a proposal that the Firm lease a copying machine. Brad Coolidge was reluctant because, as he told Bob Matusoff, he "did not believe the Firm would use the monthly minimum of 500 sheets a month." He finally acceded, and soon the Firm was using 5,000 sheets a month. Now the Firm is using over 5,000 sheets a day.

Despite the formal structure and formal appearance generally associated with the Coolidge years at the Firm, there were moments of informality and relaxation. Brad Coolidge relaxed with his daily martini at the Buz Fuz Club. During those years, the Buz Fuz Club met in a room above the Wagon Wheel Bar at the Van Cleve Hotel (now demolished, but then located at the southeast quadrant of First and Ludlow Streets). As a senior member, Brad Coolidge, Frank Hill Smith and others were daily fixtures at the round table in the Buz Fuz Club. There they played rum (a form of gin rummy). There was a ritual to this card-playing institution, and woe onto anyone who dared to sit in Brad Coolidge's chair. For that matter, woe unto anyone who dared to sit in any of the chairs at the round table, for they all were anointed for regulars whose wrath at interlopers was terrible.

An alternative to the Buz Fuz Club was the Firm's Saturday afternoon bowling ritual. Saturday mornings were part of the normal work week at Coolidge. The expectation of everyone wearing a coat and tie continued through Saturday, albeit sometimes a sport coat was permitted. Pete Wood and his wife, Joan, had a long tradition of going to Sol Friedman's restaurant at the Capri Motel on South Dixie on Saturdays for a long leisurely lunch and then spending the afternoon bowling next door at the Capri Lanes. He often took one or more of the younger lawyers with him, including from time to time Eddy Graef, Bob Matusoff, Bob Womsley, Chuck Lowe — and later Roger Makley.

One Saturday evening was going to be a very special occasion, a party to celebrate Bob Womsley's engagement to Lynn Drury. On that day, Eddy Graef had been working on an important brief, but Eddy assured his wife, Kay, that he would be home in time to make the gala evening. He also vowed that he would not go to the Capri with Pete Wood for the usual Saturday afternoon of bowling and bourbon. As promised, by six o'clock that evening he was home, in his gray flannel suit highlighted by his Williams College tie. He announced that after long hours of grueling work he had finished his legal brief and was ready to go to the party. Kay looked at him and reportedly said, "Don't you think you should take off those red and green shoes and take them back to the bowling alley?"

Brad Coolidge loved the practice of law and, in many ways, lived the practice of law, but there was another side of him. He also loved his home in Oakwood and his farm in Washington Township.

Coolidge and his wife Betty lived at 228 Southview Road in Oakwood. Coolidge will always be associated with his Southview home, but his Oakwood presence will always be preserved by Coolidge Drive, a lovely street starting at Park Road and running south to Peach Orchard. This street was named for Brad Coolidge by Horace Huffman, Sr., when Mr. Huffman was developing farm land west of Far Hills into residential lots.

For the most part, Brad Coolidge maintained a stern formal presence even at home. He always wore his coat and tie. The evening cocktail, or two, was an integral part of Brad's formal evening. He had one — or two or three — drinks before sitting down for dinner. Brad very often lived the maxim he oft expressed: "Scotch & Eat." No one started to eat at the Coolidge family dining table until everyone was seated and fully served; then there would be a formal commencement of dinner.

Coolidge lived on Southview during Prohibition. As carefully prepared at home as in his legal practice, Coolidge made sure that he had a Scotch preservation plan -- he constructed a false wall in the house and behind that false wall he maintained his supply of Scotch. In his later years, Coolidge often had Pete Wood drive him to Kentucky to buy a supply of his favorite Crabbie blended Scotch whiskey (Scotch was not Pete Wood's favorite drink. Pete Wood insisted on precise Manhattans: three parts bourbon, one part sweet vermouth, straight up.)

Coolidge also had a farm containing approximately 150 acres at the southwest quadrant of Wilmington Pike and Alex-Bell Road (State Route 725). Brad Coolidge and George Henry Wood (Brad Coolidge's brother-in-law and Pete Wood's father) had purchased, as tenants in common, the 113 acre tract for $6,405 at a sheriff's sale in a 1934 partition action (Deed Book 736, Page 254). Later, on April 30, 1935, they acquired the 31.45 acre tract from John Bradford (Deed Book 756, Page 530). Still later, on July 14, 1941, George H. Wood transferred his undivided one-half interest in the farm to Brad Coolidge, as recorded in Deed Book 941, Page 240.

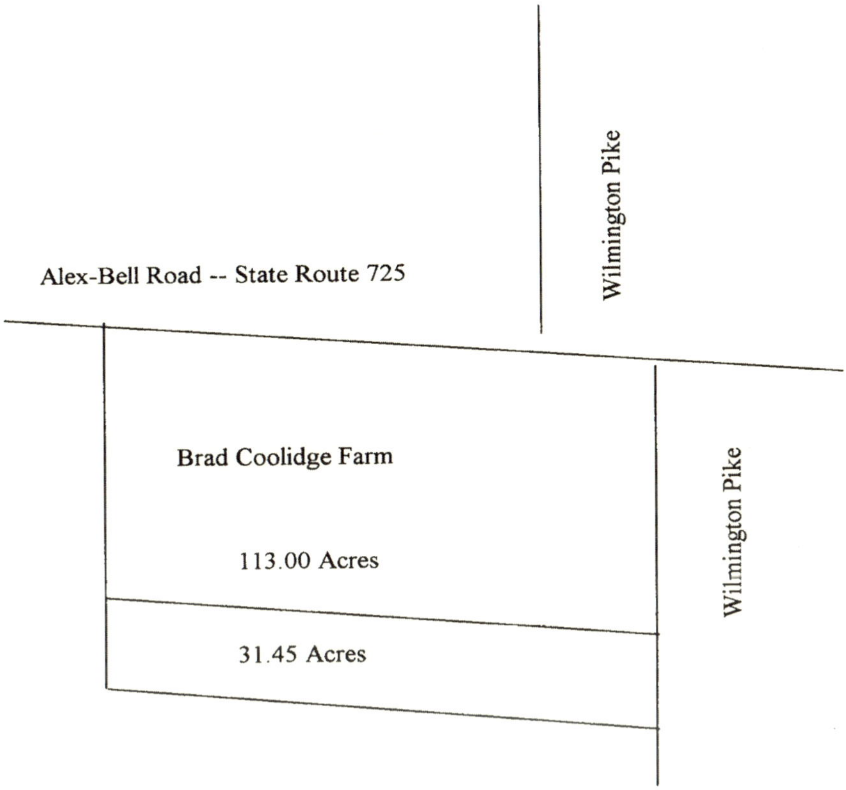

The farm, at the southeast quadrant of the intersection of Alex-Bell Road (Route 725) and Wilmington Pike, was called the "Pig Farm" within the family. There Brad Coolidge had hired hands or tenant farmers grow a variety of fruits and vegetables.

Even when he visited his farm, Brad Coolidge was true to his formal self, dressed in a suit and tie even as he proudly showed off his asparagus and sweet corn. Coolidge sold the farm to Arthur Stock on October 31, 1952, as recorded in Deed Book 1544, Page 433. The sales price was approximately $50,000 and Brad Coolidge thought he had cashed in the big chips. Now, of course, that area is in the midst of a major residential and commercial development as Wilmington Pike, Sugarcreek Township, and Bellbrook became fully integrated into the greater Dayton metropolitan community.

LAW OFFICES

COOLIDGE, WALL & WOOD

GEM CITY SAVINGS BUILDING

DAYTON, OHIO 45402

JOSEPH BRADFORD COOLIDGE
HUGH E. WALL, JR.
PEIRCE WOOD
ROBERT B. MATUSOFF
ROBERT B. WOMSLEY
JOHN C. LOMBARD
CHARLES D. LOWE

January 21,1965.

In 1962, Brad Coolidge celebrated the 50th anniversary of his admission to the bar. The Firm commissioned Lloyd Ostendorf, the Dayton painter renowned for his paintings and scholarship on Abraham Lincoln, to paint an oil portrait of Joseph Bradford Coolidge. In addition, all of the Firm lawyers signed a special plaque recognizing the event.

In the early sixties, two events triggered the decline of Coolidge's health. While on a trip to Washington, D.C., with Bob Matusoff on behalf of Loren M. Berry, Brad Coolidge caught a cold that may have later degraded to pneumonia. In addition, the lingering effects of cataract surgery affected his eyesight. Yet he persevered by conducting his practice from his home on Southview. Everyday at 3:00 p.m., Bob Womsley would call Mrs. Coolidge and ask "Is Mr. Coolidge up to meeting today?" If he was, Bob Womsley would take the mail and any pending legal documents to Brad Coolidge's house at about 5:30 p.m. On arrival, Brad Coolidge would fix two scotch drinks and discuss with Bob the day's activities at the office. Bob Womsley would leave the mail and legal documents with Brad Coolidge and his blue pencil, and pick up his work from the previous day. Throughout this time period, Brad Coolidge desperately wanted to stay connected to the Firm, attending to his own responsibilities, but primarily cheering on the efforts of the other lawyers at the Firm.

By 1964 Brad Coolidge reluctantly recognized that he needed to move aside and the Firm needed to move forward. Brad Coolidge certainly felt a sense of history and a sense of the Firm's future as he ceded his complete autonomy and entered into a formal partnership with Hugh E. Wall, Jr., Pete Wood, and Bob Matusoff. Brad Coolidge transferred to the new partnership his legal practice and

Joseph Bradford Coolidge
1886-1965

all of his tangible personal property at the Firm, as evidenced in his Last Will and Testament, dated October 10, 1964. His health was failing, and not long after executing his estate planning documents, Brad Coolidge died on February 15, 1965. On May 5, 1973, his widow, Betty Peirce Coolidge, died. They are both buried in Woodland Cemetery.

CHAPTER FOUR

THE HUGH E. WALL, JR., ROBERT B. MATUSOFF, ROBERT B. WOMSLEY & JOHN C. LOMBARD ERA

1966-1976

The ten years between the death of Brad Coolidge and the retirement of Hugh E. Wall, Jr., produced a critical transition in the Firm, in personnel and in development of the Firm's specialized areas of practicc. During this period, Wood would be reducing his active practice in order to retire, and new lawyers would be added, most of whom remain active in the Firm to this day. I would be one of these. For purposes of this book, this begins the era of first names.

Brad Coolidge had practiced at the Firm for over fifty years and was a major presence in the Dayton legal and business community. He had hired well and by this time the other lawyers had developed their own expertise and following. Nevertheless, given the extraordinary client relationships enjoyed by Brad Coolidge, his death engendered some uncertainty as the Firm confronted its future; however, Coolidge's protégés transformed the challenges of his death into the opportunities of the future. Besides Pete Wood and Hugh Wall, Jr., the composition of the Firm was generally young, foretelling long careers for the partners to practice and develop the Firm. Bob Matusoff, Bob Womsley, and John Lombard were in their early 40s. C. Terry Johnson and Ron Pretekin were younger yet.

After Brad Coolidge's death, the Firm made three important revisions to its letterhead. It incorporated the new zip code of 45402 in place of the old postal zone designation of "Dayton 2, Ohio." The following two additions were more important:

- Joseph Bradford Coolidge
  (1912-1965)

- Area Code 513
  223-8177

The first change gave recognition to Brad Coolidge's fifty-three years of practice as a lawyer in Dayton, Ohio. The other change reflected the first time in the history of the Firm that the Firm put its telephone number on its letterhead. The absence of a law firm's telephone number on its letterhead seems almost unfathomable in today's communication and marketing world, but that practice probably reflected the special culture of the Brad Coolidge era. Certainly, it reflects the pace of the practice of law at that time.

In 1968, Bob Matusoff registered with Western Union the special cable address code named **"Coollaw."** Cable addresses were common then and many law firms listed their cable address on their letterhead. Western Union established cable addresses to facilitate communication between companies that used the system on a regular basis. There were Cable Directories which listed firms (nationwide and worldwide) with their cable addresses. In many ways, the cable address worked like an e-mail address as a dedicated reception point for messages directed to the company. The Firm's **"Coollaw"** cable address has segued almost seamlessly into the Firm's Internet address. When domain registration first became available, the Firm reserved the **"Coollaw"** name and subsequently developed its website at **www.coollaw.com**.

The Firm needed to move out of the Callahan Building (or the Gem Savings Building as it was being called in the late 1950s and 1960s), which could no longer provide the space or the amenities for the Firm to meet its growing needs. Gene and Virginia Kettering had been discussing the possibility of constructing a new tower for the Winters National Bank, but that planning process was moving more slowly than the Firm's progress and needs could accommodate. As the Firm was considering its options, Bob Matusoff and Hugh Wall, Jr., heard that Apple, Moody & Woodley, a partnership consisting of Bill Apple, Paul Moody, and Ralph Woodley, was going to put up a new six-story office building at 33 West First Street, the northeast quadrant of First and Ludlow Streets. The lower floors had already been leased to IBM Corporation, but there was space on the sixth floor where Apple, Moody and Woodley proposed that the Firm could have the five-thousand square feet fronting First Street.

The building was called the "IBM Building" (now known as the "Soin International Building") since IBM was the lead tenant, but the Firm's lease for its space was actually with Apple, Moody and Woodley, the original owner. The building would later be sold to IBM Corporation after Thomas J. Watson, Jr., the President of IBM, liked what he saw when he came out to Dayton for the building's dedication. Perhaps Tom Watson also liked the fact that the IBM Building was almost in the backyard of the family home of his mother, Jeannette Kittredge, who lived at 217 North Ludlow when she married Thomas J. Watson, Sr., in 1913. If the Kittredge family home was not on the exact IBM Building site, as the story has often been told, it certainly would have been directly across the street, immediately south of the Dayton Women's Club at 225 North Ludlow. As Bill Apple recounted the story of the building's sale, he and Tom Watson had a handshake deal on the sale of the building and never even reduced it to writing. "We just met at the title company and exchanged the deed for cash. Tom Watson's word was good enough for me."

Next in importance to securing the lease was planning for the leasehold improvements, the interior design, and the furniture and fixtures. From a number of sources the Firm had heard of Alan Ferry & Co., an interior design firm out of Atlanta, Georgia. Their recent projects had included the design work and furniture acquisition for the Trust Department of Winters Bank, the Executive Offices for the L.M. Berry Company, and the Executive Offices at the Reynolds + Reynolds Company. A strong confirmation by John Berry of his satisfaction was enough for Bob Matusoff and Hugh Wall. The Alan Ferry group would do the design work for the Firm's new offices in the IBM Building. The Alan Ferry firm a masterful design and decorating program at the Firm which was admired by all — except perhaps Pete Wood who needled his partners by asserting that he could practice off an orange crate. His office was ultimately

IBM Building
Soin International Building
33 West First Street
Dayton, Ohio

determined to be one of the most attractive — since he refused to express any personal preferences, giving the decorators free reign.

The move from the Gem Savings Building to the IBM Building marked the first time the Firm was not located on Main Street, and the first time the Firm did not move within a block of the courthouse. More importantly, it dramatically changed the atmosphere of the Firm, transforming the look from a Spartan 1920s parlor to a walnut panelled Athenaeum. The threadbare rugs and steel shelving of the old office gave way to oriental rugs and walnut cabinets in the new office. Through it all, it was Bob Matusoff who was sometimes paving and sometimes bulldozing the path of the future, to make sure that the new offices had all the accoutrements of success. Conference Room I was designed to give Firm members a sort of home court advantage. The transformation was a success and in subsequent years several proposals to move again, to larger or newer space, were rejected out of reluctance to give up the Ferry-designed lobby, offices, and conference rooms.

When the actual move came, it was more of a U-Haul move than a Mayflower move. All of the lawyers put on their jeans and rolled up their sleeves to pack up the library and restack the books in their new location. Attired like a longshoreman in his white T-shirt and blue jeans, Pete Wood was probably wishing that he could just stay in steerage and practice off an orange crate. Nevertheless, he and the others went along with it and completed the library and then the file room, and the Firm was ready to open for business in its new suite.

Almost simultaneously with the move from the Gem Savings Building to the IBM Building, the Firm added Roger Makley. Prior to joining the Firm to become the heir apparent to Pete Wood's litigation practice, Roger had worked in a

Senator John Glenn and Roger Makley

number of federal government positions culminating in his appointment as the U.S. Attorney for the Southern District of Ohio. After he joined the Firm, he served as the part-time U.S. Magistrate for the Southern District of Ohio until the position became a full-time position. His academic background was impressive. Roger had three degrees from Georgetown University, making him the biggest Hoya in the Dayton community and a dramatic presence in the Firm.

In the 1960's, there were no "departments" within the Firm, and entering lawyers were thrust into all areas of the law, the prevailing wisdom being that a new lawyer needed broad experience to be effective. The attitude towards training new lawyers, typical of firms at the time, was summarized by Bob Womsley: "Drop them in the deep end of the pool and see if they can swim." During those days the Firm hired bright young lawyers, believing that the Firm's practice and the individual's personal interests would take him in a particular direction over time. Invariably that worked – or at least it worked as long as the direction of the practice was acceptable to the individual lawyer. Consequently, none of the next few lawyers knew their future areas of practice before they arrived at the Firm.

One of the lawyers who thrived in this environment was Ronald S. Pretekin who had started in a general practice and then migrated over a long career to become a bankruptcy specialist. Ron Pretekin, the son of Maurice and Jane Ellen Pretekin, was born on April 19, 1942. He joined the Firm in 1966 after he was graduated from the University of Oklahoma and the University of Michigan Law School.

At about the same time, William H. "Bud" Seall joined the Firm. He was born on January 14, 1943, and was graduated from St. Mary's University (Minnesota) and from Notre Dame Law School. Bud's early work with Bob Matusoff took him primarily to corporate and securities work for publicly held companies. Following closely behind Bud Seall was Jonas Joe Gruenberg, born in Tarnopol, Poland (now re-designated as part of the Ukraine), on December 5, 1945, and graduating from the University of Pennsylvania in 1967 and Vanderbilt Law School in 1970. Joe Gruenberg worked in a variety of areas but generally gravitated towards working with Bob Womsley and Pete Wood, who continued as the pre-eminent real estate lawyer in Dayton, particularly in the area of highway appropriation cases.

Presently there are still a few lawyers at the Firm who have had the good fortune of working with Pete Wood. Roger Makley has told the tale of trying a case with Pete Wood as his co-counsel just after Roger joined the Firm. Like some of the tough smart lawyers you might see on the side of a bus, Pete Wood and Roger Makley were pursuing a personal injury and wrongful death claim arising out of an auto accident. Pete was both tutoring Roger and transferring to Roger case responsibility. Of course, Pete tutored best with bravado and bourbon. When they got to the final argument, Roger, fortified by Pete's tutoring, was nearly overcome by the emotion of the facts of the case. Roger completed his presentation to the jury with tears streaming down his face as he pleaded with the jury to compensate their clients for the tragedy that had befallen them. Roger then returned to the counsel table, wiping the tears off of his face, only to have Pete Wood lean over and whisper, "Nice touch."

Pete Wood phased out of his active practice in the early 1970s and then moved to Melbourne, Florida. At the age of 56, Pete Wood prepared the very lengthy Florida Bar Examination application, which required detailed information on his every address along with a comprehensive background presentation. In a remarkable intellectual feat for someone out of law school for over 30 years, Pete successfully passed the Florida Bar Exam. In Melbourne, now more as an avocation but with no less intensity, Pete pursued those zoning and civic interest cases which appealed to him, including serving with the Florida Supreme Court as a Hearing Referee on attorney disciplinary matters.

The lawyers in the Firm who had the opportunity to work with Pete Wood had a wonderful opportunity to see an intellectual maverick at work, a legal genius who was never thwarted because the desired result did not fit within the hornbook solution. Pete would find another way. It was said of Pete that he would not just connect the dots from A to B, but go from A to C to D to get to B, or that Pete could find a shorter distance between two points than a straight line. When anyone needed a creative mind to resolve a complex problem, Pete Wood would be called upon. His creativity will always be the bar against which other lawyers are measured. When Pete Wood died on June 8, 1987, the Firm lost one of its most creative legal thinkers. Peirce "Pete" Wood is interred next to a monumental rock in a sylvan setting at Woodland Cemetery in Dayton.

By 1972, the Firm had outgrown its original space in the IBM Building and added approximately 3,000 square feet, which meant that the Firm had the front half of the IBM Building. The Firm did not employ Alan Ferry for the expansion and modified some of the more costly features of the original design, using stained pine, for example, instead of continuing the walnut walls and molding of the original space. This led Roger Makley to coin the phrase “King’s Row” for the original walnut paneled offices on the sixth floor fronting First Street and the phrase “Back Porch” for the offices with the stained pine molding in the rear along Ludlow Street, offices then occupied by the newest associates. It would be a phrase that would endure through multiple expansions and lawyer transitions.

Jeffry A. Melnick came to the Firm after interning with Ohio Senator William Saxbe’s office in Washington, D.C. Jeff was born on June 3, 1946, grew up in Chicago, Illinois, and was graduated from Carleton College in Northfield, Minnesota in 1968 and from Yale Law School in 1971. At Yale, Jeff was in the same student body with a large number of public figures, including President Bill Clinton and Senator Hillary Rodham Clinton. Because of his interest in corporate law, Jeff Melnick generally worked with Bob Matusoff during his early years, concentrating on securities work and general corporate work.

Hugh E. Wall, III, was born on November 5, 1946, and was, of course, the son of Hugh E. Wall, Jr. Being the son of the senior partner was a benefit for him, but it carried with it the burden of high expectations. Hugh E. Wall, III, was graduated from the University of St. Thomas in St. Paul, Minnesota, and then from University of Cincinnati Law School. As he joined the Firm, he worked with the clients of his father and provided a continuity of representation over the succeeding years.

In June 1973, I came to the Firm from Arent, Fox, Kintner, Plotkin & Kahn in Washington, D.C., where I had been stationed during my four years as a captain in the U.S. Army Judge Advocate General’s Corps. At that time, the JAG Corps’ approach to new lawyer training was not

Army Court of Military Review
United States v. Lt. William L. Calley
December 4, 1972

Left to Right: George W. Latimer, Judge Wayne Alley, Capt. J. Houston Gordon, Capt. M. Douglas Deitchler, Capt. Merle F. Wilberding, Capt. Robert C. Roth, Lt. Col. Ronald M. Holdaway
CBS Evening News Courtroom Sketch

markedly different from the Firm's "deep water" approach — I had briefed and argued on behalf of the Government the appeal of the court-martial conviction of Lt. William L. Calley in the My Lai (Vietnam) Massacre. Born on March 8, 1944, I had degrees from St. Mary's University (Minnesota), Notre Dame Law School, George Washington University, and the University of Dayton. When I arrived at the Firm, the general economic climate had ebbed a little and although the corporate legal work was holding its own, it was not expanding. Consequently, I worked with Hugh E. Wall, Jr., on tax work and with Bob Womsley on a series of real estate projects.

With five new associate lawyers all on board with the Firm by June of 1973, and with Pete Wood having retired, the Firm was left with a net lawyer count of twelve. It would stay at that number for almost four years, throughout the remainder of Hugh E. Wall, Jr.'s active practice.

It was during the period of the late 1950s and extending through the early 1970s that the Firm developed its securities business with a number of publicly-held companies, including Huffy, Philips Industries, Zimmer Homes, and Ponderosa. The first S-1 public offering was done for Horace Huffman as he took Huffy public with its bicycle manufacturing business.

Soon after that, Jesse Philips, an Executive Vice President at the Home Store, came to the Firm for help in an acquisition that he wanted to pursue. In response, Bob Matusoff worked with Jesse Philips on his acquisition of Jalousies of Ohio, Inc., a small manufacturer of door and window components for the mobile home industry. Jesse Philips changed the name of the company to "Philips Industries, Inc." and had its first public offering through the Ohio Company. Catching the wave of the mobile home market spurt of the 1960s, Philips next had a public offering through Merrill Lynch. It soon became one of the hottest stocks in the market place and was listed on the New York Stock Exchange.

That success attracted Paul Zimmer who came to the Firm for help from Bob Matusoff in acquiring Princess Homes, a mobile home manufacturer located in Selinsgrove, Pennsylvania. The same pattern of multiple primary and secondary stock offerings enabled Zimmer Homes to develop an empire in the mobile home industry and in the process enabled the Firm to develop a national presence in the securities field.

That securities experience served the Firm well and served Ponderosa well. Indeed, Ponderosa experienced a meteoric rise that coincided with the growth of the Firm. The original Ponderosa concept came from Dan Lasater, a dynamic young entrepreneur whose family had migrated from Letona, Arkansas, to Kokomo, Indiana, where he first worked at McDonalds. At the age of twenty, he started a Scotty's hamburger business, and at the age of twenty-two, he opened the first Ponderosa restaurant. A few years later, his negotiations with an Ohio Burger Chef franchisee brought him to the Dayton law firm of Office & Office. This was while the Firm still occupied the twelfth and part of the eleventh floor of the Gem Savings Building. Jerry Office, Sr., and Jerry Office, Jr., shared the eleventh floor with the Firm.

In December 1969, Jerry Office, Jr., at the age of twenty-seven, became CEO and President of Ponderosa with Dan Lasater remaining as Executive Vice President of Operations. Through a series of public offerings, hard work, and a robust stock market, Ponderosa made its mark in America and its stock prices soared. After a couple of years Lasater left with a reported $ 30 million of stock profits. Later he returned to his roots in Arkansas where he entwined himself into the Arkansas political world of Governor Bill Clinton and his brother, Roger Clinton.

Ponderosa was a unique Dayton community asset, and so was another developing client at the Firm in a very different market. The *Ohio Players*, an R & B group whose members all had roots in Dayton, had risen to the top of the charts in the R & B market, with more than a dozen gold records and several platinum records, including *Love Roller Coaster*, *Fire*, and *Honey*. Since the 1970s, the Firm has had the opportunity to work with them on a variety of issues relating to taxes and the entertainment industry, especially during the 1990s when their music made a dramatic comeback under two of the original members, James "Diamond" Williams and LeRoy "Sugar" Bonner, who continue to lead the group. Sugar's presence always captivated the attention of everyone with his dazzling jewelry and sartorial splender.

Besides the securities and entertainment work, the Firm was rapidly expanding its services in other areas. John Lombard was the key to developing a long relationship with Kettering Medical Center and its presidents, including George Nelson, Marlowe Shaffner, Bob Willett, and Frank Perez. Bob Womsley was developing a strong following in the real estate community with, among others, Jerv Janney, Dayton

Hydraulic and Frank Hill Smith and their portfolio of industrial real estate, with George Henkle and Mike Schueler and their portfolio of farms between Dayton and Cincinnati, and with George Smith and Wilbur Johnston and their portfolio of thoroughbreds and horse farms.

The early 1970s brought enormous political uproar, centering on the Watergate Investigation of President Richard M. Nixon. The Watergate story seemed to consume the media and the populace. The Dayton community and the Firm were not excluded from some tangential involvement in the ensuing Watergate Investigation. At the Firm's golf outing at Moraine Country Club in July 1973, Hugh E. Wall, Jr., was called from the golf course to consult with Loren M. Berry who that day was explaining to the Senate Watergate Committee his contributions to Richard Nixon's presidential campaign. Later, North Carolina Senator Sam Ervin, the chairman of the Senate Watergate Committee, spoke at one of the noon luncheons of the Dayton Bar Association. Finally, at a Firm dinner at the Dayton Country Club on August 8, 1974, Bob Matusoff recessed the dinner early so that all of the lawyers could go into the adjoining Bar & Grill and watch President Richard M. Nixon announce on television his resignation from office.

This period also brought the beginning of the technology movement in the practice of law. When the Firm first moved to 33 West First Street in 1968, the telephone system was virtually the same as had existed for the preceding forty years. The telephone switchboard was in a large console with interconnects between the four outside telephone lines (accessed by four matched pairs of connecting cords) to the twenty extensions throughout the office. When the red light would signal an incoming telephone call, the Firm's telephone operator would plug one cord into the receiving line and answer the phone and then connect that call to the appropriate person by plugging the other cord into his extension; she would then announce the call, and complete the circuit. A separate intercom system enabled intra office communications among the lawyers and staff.

The Firm also had a precursor of the fax machine, a telecopier machine that very slowly transmitted documents, but only if the intended recipient had a compatible machine to receive the document. Consequently, documents were rarely transmitted by this process, save for the urgent communications relating to the securities work the Firm was doing with the New York law firms and the printing related to these public offerings or SEC registrations.

One of the big changes during this period was the switchover in the Firm's file system and time-keeping record system. In April 1973, the Firm adopted an alpha-numeric client system which enabled the Firm to implement both a new file system and a new, remote-batch electronic time-keeping system. Lawyers' time sheets were no longer simply thrown in each client's file, as had been the practice in prior years. Instead, the data from these time sheets were input into a IBM MT/ST automatic typewriter creating a tape which was then sent to a processing office in New York. Invoices were prepared in a similar remote batch processing method. It may seem antiquated now, but it was an extraordinary step forward at the time, and put the Firm in the forefront of the legal technology process. Little did anyone know how fast this area of office technology would advance during the ensuing twenty-five years.

After the death of Brad Coolidge, Hugh E. Wall, Jr., had become to many the icon of the Firm. He had an enormous presence in the Dayton business community, as his reputation for tax and business advice grew. More than anything, he was respected for his wisdom, his concern for all clients, and his civility. He consistently took the high road on all legal projects, even in those adversarial proceedings when his opponent failed to do so.

During the post-Coolidge era, Hugh E. Wall, Jr. was heavily involved with the expansion and structuring of the L. M. Berry & Company. For the first fifty years, Loren M. Berry operated the Yellow Page business as a sole proprietorship, even during those years when the individual income tax rates were virtually confiscatory. He continued that ownership structure almost as a badge of honor, in part because he believed it was his patriotic duty to pay taxes to the same government that had provided him his opportunity to succeed. As the business grew and the business became the owner of office properties in multiple states, he accepted that he needed to incorporate.

Because the L. M. Berry & Company had already been in business more than fifty years, incorporating the business was a major transaction — so large that a revenue ruling and technical advice were necessary from the Internal Revenue Service to insure that no taxes were incurred in the initial incorporation process and, later, in the continued use of the cash basis method of accounting. Hugh E. Wall, Jr., brilliantly quarterbacked these strategies, enlisting the help of Charles W. Davis and Frederic L. Hahn from the old Hopkins, Sutter law firm in Chicago for strategic and technical support. He drew still more support within the

Firm, from Bob Matusoff in the earlier transaction and from me in the later transaction. Ultimately, the Berry Company prevailed on all fronts and continued its marvelous growth in the Yellow Page directory business.

In addition to the Berry representation, Hugh Wall, Jr., counseled a large number of businesses and organizations as they worked their way through the challenges and opportunities in their respective lines of business. He had succeeded to Brad Coolidge's position on the Board of Directors of the Reynolds + Reynolds Co. and continued in that position until his own retirement. He also served as a director on numerous privately held corporations and as trustee for the University of Dayton and six charitable foundations.

Hugh E. Wall, Jr. retired from the Firm on December 31, 1976, after thirty-five years of practice with the Firm, just three months short of his sixty-fifth birthday. He continued as "Of Counsel" for many years after that, sharing his wisdom and counsel with the Firm lawyers who came after him. Even after moving to Naples, Florida, in the late 1970s, he continued his close association with the Firm, the University of Dayton (serving on its Board of Trustees), and its School of Law (being a significant fund raiser for the construction of its new building). Hugh E. Wall, Jr., died on January 24, 2001, with his life being celebrated by the Mass of Christian Burial at the Church of the Holy Angels on January 27, 2001, before being interred next to Clare Aull Wall at Calvary Cemetery in Dayton.

CHAPTER FIVE

THE CURRENT ERA

1977 – 2003

January 1, 1977, marked another significant transition point in the history of the Firm. The final day of the previous year was the final day of Hugh E. Wall, Jr.'s presence as a principal in the Firm. It also marked the start of the Firm's operations under a corporate structure, Coolidge, Wall, Matusoff, Womsley & Lombard Co., L.P.A.

The transition from a general partnership to a professional corporation involved a long process of evaluation and preparation, intended to coincide with the retirement of Hugh Wall. The prior general partnership had no retirement plan and no one wanted to create a pension plan that would permit a major principal in the Firm to participate for only one or two years.

The ability to adopt corporate pension plans and provide other corporate benefits was a major impetus for switching to a corporate form of operation and governance, but there were other reasons that weighed in favor of a corporate form. Everyone believed that the Firm stood on the threshold of a major business expansion. If that occurred, the general partnership structure would produce recurring difficulties in admitting new partners and appropriately recognizing those partners who generated the growth of the Firm. The addition of each new partner would necessitate an adjustment of other partners' percentages in sharing of profits and losses. Moreover, a corporate structure would more appropriately adjust to the changing dynamics of Firm leadership and revenue production.

Under the corporate structure, there would be an Executive Committee elected annually by members of the Firm instead of stipulated by a partnership agreement. There would also be an elected Compensation Committee to allocate compensation and award bonuses, without the year-end toasts of brandy of the Brad Coolidge era. Finally, there would be an elected Firm president. Since the adoption of the corporate structure, Firm members who have served as president include Bob Matusoff, Bob Womsley, John Lombard, Jeff Melnick, and Steve Herbert.

Back in 1977, the Firm had consisted of only twelve lawyers, including eleven partners (as the shareholders were commonly called). This structure caused Pete Wood to suggest wryly to Joe Gruenberg that on our 1977 letterhead, we "looked a little bit like a South American army, all generals."

LAW OFFICES

COOLIDGE, WALL, MATUSOFF, WOMSLEY & LOMBARD CO., L. P. A.

SUITE 600, IBM BUILDING

DAYTON, OHIO 45402

ROBERT B. MATUSOFF
ROBERT B. WOMSLEY
JOHN C. LOMBARD
C. TERRY JOHNSON
RONALD S. PRETEKIN
ROGER J. MAKLEY
WILLIAM H. SEALL
JONAS J. GRUENBERG
JEFFRY A. MELNICK
MERLE F. WILBERDING

HUGH E. WALL, III

AREA CODE 513
223-8177
CABLE: COOL-LAW

JOSEPH BRADFORD COOLIDGE
(1912-1965)

—

HUGH E. WALL, JR.
OF COUNSEL

PEIRCE WOOD
SPECIAL COUNSEL

February 18, 1977

The Firm was still in the same sixth floor space in the IBM Building as after its 1972 expansion, and that space accommodated only twelve lawyers. Over the next five years, through 1981, the Firm would double its space and take the entire sixth floor. This more than doubled the number of lawyer offices to accommodate Firm growth.

During that five year span, the Firm prospered as the business cycle improved. The Firm started an aggressive recruiting program and hired a number of new associates, most directly out of the law schools, and commenced a permanent summer clerk program for first and second year law students. In addition there were recruiting efforts aimed at local sources. From these efforts came several of the Firm's future leaders.

Glenn L. Bower joined the Firm in 1977 after first working across town at Smith & Schnacke. Originally, he grew up in Silver Spring, Maryland, before heading off to college. He was graduated from Penn State University and Harvard Law School.

J. Stephen Herbert grew up in Dayton. He was graduated from Yale University and then the University of Virginia Law School in 1978. Steve clerked for the Firm after his first year of law school and then returned after graduation. Upon his arrival, he tended to work on real estate projects under Bob Womsley, thereby establishing the basis for his successful career as a real estate lawyer.

One of the Firm's recruiting trips to Duke Law School identified Fred A. Ungerman who accepted invitations to visit and then join the Firm. Fred was originally from Philadelphia and was graduated from Grove City College in Pennsylvania.

By this time, the Firm was starting to gel informally into practice groups, but there were no department assignments and certainly no absolutes. The Firm was still

Fred A. Ungerman, Jr.

looking for new associates to identify their own strengths and "find" the area of law that they liked and that best suited them.

In January 1983 it was announced that Bob Matusoff was leaving the Firm. In many ways this was a dramatic event in the Firm and in the business community. Bob was a natural leader and a powerful force in any transaction or negotiation, and certainly within the Firm. When Brad Coolidge died, Bob Matusoff was there with Hugh Wall to pick up the leadership of the Firm, bring it through times of economic and Firm uncertainty, and lead it to the next level. Bob Matusoff was a primary force in moving the Firm from the Gem Savings Building (as the Callahan Building was then known) to the IBM Building, modernizing the technology, and enhancing the Firm's image in the business community. In the process he developed a successful and lucrative securities practice with a group of publicly held companies, including Ponderosa, Huffy, Zimmer Homes, and Philips Industries.

Indeed, in many ways, Bob Matusoff may have operated the Firm in the image and likeness of Brad Coolidge. At the same time, the Brad Coolidge style of law firm management was being reconsidered not just at the Firm, but throughout the country. There were a number of vectoring forces pushing this movement. Law firms had more and more younger lawyers — younger lawyers who wanted to participatc in firm management and firm revenue, and wanted to participate sooner rather than later. These younger attorneys themselves may have been influenced by the social and political upheaval of the 1960s, as the youth of our country was challenging the traditions and dictates of the older generation. At the same time, clients were more discerning in their relationships and blind loyalties were yielding to increasing perceptions (albeit erroneous) of the fungible market value of legal representation.

Over time these internal political forces challenged the existing tenets of leadership and governance of the Firm. None of the beliefs or visions in these discussions was inherently wrong. They were simply different. Finally, they resolved themselves with a mutually acceptable agreement between the Firm and Bob Matusoff that enabled him to continue his practice in a separate office in the Winters Bank Tower (now known as the Kettering Tower). Although the logic and business wisdom of the conclusion was accepted, it was a difficult process for everyone. However, the rear view mirror has demonstrated that all parties have continued their respective legal practices successfully, albeit on independent pathways. Bob Matusoff later did class action securities work in Cincinnati. In 1995, he joined John Dupps and the Dupps Company where he has served as Vice President – Management Counsel. The Dupps Company is a long time Firm client going back to the days when Pete Wood had represented Jack Dupps, the father of John Dupps.

On January 11, 1983, the Firm officially changed its name to "Coolidge, Wall, Womsley & Lombard," asked Bob Womsley to assume the Firm's leadership, and pursued its new direction with a regenerated enthusiasm. Almost immediately, the Firm made two personnel decisions. First, Glenn L. Bower and Steve Herbert were elected to become shareholders, and, second, Sam Warwar was hired away from Smith & Schnacke. Sam Warwar had grown up in Dayton. His father, Elias Warwar, had operated a specialty men's tailor shop for many years. After graduating with a B.A. from the Ohio State University, Sam Warwar earned his J.D. from University of Dayton School of Law. From there he went to University of Florida and earned the degree of Master of Law

The Lewis B. Gunckel Desk

From left to right: Glenn Bower, Merle Wilberding, John Lombard, Roger Makley, Robert Womsley, Jeffry Melnick

in Tax. Upon his arrival at the Firm, he did exclusively tax work, eventually becoming Chairman of the Tax Department.

Soon after, in 1984, R. Scott Blackburn was hired by the Firm to be primarily responsible for estate planning and probate administration. Scott Blackburn was graduated from Ohio University (B.B.A.), University of Cincinnati (M.B.A.) and University of Toledo (J.D.). Prior to joining the Firm, he worked in the Trust Department at the Third National Bank & Trust Company prior to its merger into Society Bank, which was later merged into Key Bank. On August 1, 1985, Richard A. Schwartz, began working at the Firm after having started his career at Smith & Schnacke. Rick was graduated from University of Toledo (B.A.) and the Ohio State University School of Law (J.D.). At the Firm, he joined the Corporate Department.

The litigation services of the Firm were expanded significantly when Robert P. Bartlett, Jr., joined the Firm in the late 1980s after a long career at Estabrook, Finn & McKee, including during the initial period after the Estabrook firm merged into the Porter, Wright law firm headquartered in Columbus. As a son of an American Baptist minister, Bob Bartlett received a special scholarship to Denison University from which he graduated in 1960. Later, he was graduated from the Law School at the Ohio State University in 1963.

J. Stephen Herbert

During this period, the Firm was involved in some major transactions in the Dayton business community. In June 1983, the holding company of Winters Bank, with its $1.6 million in assets, merged into Bank One, creating Ohio's largest bank holding company. In many ways this bank merger was a bellwether signaling major changes in the banking industry and, for that matter, major changes in the law firm industry. New specialties had to be added, economies of scale had to be attained, and major changes in technology had to be acquired and implemented. Times were changing very rapidly.

By the summer of 1983, the Firm had worked its way through the departure of Bob Matusoff and the merger of Winters Bank into Bank One. More changes were soon on the way. In the spring of 1986, L. M. Berry and Company, one of the nation's major provider of telephone directories and Yellow Page advertising, announced that it was merging into one of the regional "Baby Bells," Bell South Corporation, headquartered in Atlanta, Georgia. The Berry Company had been one of the largest privately held companies in the United States, starting in 1910 by Loren M. Berry in a small office in the U. B. Building, just down the hall from Brad Coolidge's office.

The Firm's legal roots in the Berry Company were broad and deep. The Berry Company's 50th year souvenir book, published in 1960, recognized Brad Coolidge as a lawyer in whom Loren Berry had great confidence. He was the first lawyer Loren Berry used and in 1960 still served as the company's primary legal counsel. After the death of Brad Coolidge, Hugh E. Wall, Jr., stepped in as the primary legal representative and served in that capacity until his retirement in 1976. His work included the transition of top management from Loren M. Berry to John W. Berry, Sr. In 1977 Bob Womsley assumed that responsibility and continued

Jonas J. Gruenberg

Robert P. Barlett, Jr.

Ronald S. Pretekin

Merle F. Wilberding

in that role through the final merger. The merger itself became effective on April 22, 1986. With that merger, the legal representation of the Berry Company literally went south to Atlanta, ending seventy-five years of continuous legal representation of a major client.

Soon another major client, Ponderosa, was having its management control and autonomy challenged. First, USACafes, led by its chairman, Sam Wyly, offered to pay $15 per share in a hostile takeover. The resulting and no doubt inevitable litigation that followed brought in Marty Lipton from the New York law firm of Wachtell-Lipton for consultation as the attack was finally settled with a reported "green mail" payment of $5 million.

Then Asher Edelman, a corporate takeover specialist (or "corporate raider"), disclosed that his group had acquired more than five per cent of the outstanding stock of Ponderosa and would be making a tender offer to acquire additional shares of Ponderosa stock sufficient to give him complete control of the Ponderosa corporation.

The alarm bells sounded as CEO Jerry Office sought to mobilize Ponderosa's army of investment bankers, lawyers, and accountants either to challenge the takeover or to maximize shareholder value. In addition, an immediate legal audit was necessary to make sure that various corporate agreements and plans operating successfully within the present management structure were strong enough to withstand the inevitable corporate cuts that accompanied a regime change. Those of us on the Ponderosa take-over project soon found ourselves spending all day, every day, at the Ponderosa corporate headquarters then located in the I. M. Pei designed building at the old Callahan Building site — so much so, that we referred to our days there as our time in "The Bunker."

The Bunker was an apt description of the strategy sessions at the corporate headquarters, for in many ways this was an economic war over shareholder value, with many of the inevitable surf and turf battles along the way. As the battle process wound down, the stock price wound up, with an agreed takeover price of $29.25 per share.

The closing for the change of control was set for January 21, 1987. The fact that there was a "change of control" played a critical role in a number of Ponderosa corporate plans and employment relationships, including the funding of the so-called "golden parachutes" for a number of top executives. On the day of the actual change of control, there was one legal team at the Firm monitoring the transfer of Ponderosa assets and control to the Asher Edelman group and another legal team at the home of Jerry Office monitoring the transfer of Ponderosa assets to those executives whose Golden Parachutes had been opened.

At about the same time as the Ponderosa take over, Bud Seall shocked everyone in the Firm when he announced that he was leaving. He decided to pursue fame and fortune in the unpredictable world of real estate financing. His departure in some ways solidified the institutionalization of the Firm, as everyone recognized that the Firm had developed its own permanent stability in the legal and business community.

This era also witnessed tremendous growth of litigation involving professional conduct and relationships, cases like the Sky Marshals and the expanded (mostly by statute) concept of white-collar crime – involving conduct that might have been considered civil fraud in past eras, but not crime. Roger Makley was in the forefront in all of these cases. In the class action "Sky Marshal" case, Roger represented the U.S. Marshals who were seeking additional compensation for the overtime they incurred in their line of duty. These

Glenn L. Bower

Sam Warwar

Richard A. Schwartz

Barbara L. Sager

federal officers were assigned as in-flight security officers, attempting to prevent or combat airplane hijackings before there were any passenger screening systems. Roger also represented David Schiebel who was criminally charged along with Marvin Warner, a former ambassador to Switzerland under President Jimmy Carter, in the 1985 collapse of the Home State Savings Bank, a state chartered thrift system that was headquartered in Cincinnati and had a major presence in Dayton.

Beginning in the late 1980s, Roger Makley represented Pete Rose in his battles with Major League Baseball and the Internal Revenue Service. This representation brought Fay Vincent, the then Deputy Commissioner of Major League Baseball, and Pete Rose to the Firm's offices on several but separate occasions as both sides pursued a determination and resolution of the charges and evidence. Not since the original Colonel Harlan Sanders visited the Firm in the mid-1970s had a client's presence caused the stir that it did when Pete Rose was scheduled for an appointment.

The changing nature of the practice of law throughout the country, the transactional events within the Firm during the 1980s and the dramatic growth of the Firm all contributed to the transformation of the Firm's practice into various substantive practice groups. Lawyers within the Firm and clients outside the Firm accepted these changes as an improved method of the delivery of legal services. Hiring is by a Legal Services Committee, but now conducted on a department basis, to build up the special expertise necessary to take on the new legal projects coming over the horizon.

Lawyers in the Corporate Department of the Firm who have become shareholders include Richard A. Schwartz (B.A., University of Toledo, J.D., Ohio State University), and Barbara L. Sager (B.A., University of Cincinnati, J.D. Harvard University).

Timothy D. Hoffman

David N. Reed

John C. Chambers

M. Shannon Martin

The Real Estate Department includes the following shareholders: John C. Chambers (B.A., Ohio University, M.P.P., University of Michigan, J.D., University of Dayton), David N. Reed (B.A., Dartmouth University, J.D., University of Notre Dame) and M. Shannon Martin (B.A. John Carroll University, J.D. Cleveland-Marshall).

Shareholders in the Labor Department are Jeffrey A. Mullins (B.A. & J.D., University of Dayton), and Nicholas E. Davis, Jr. (B.A., Kent State University, J.D., University of Dayton).

The Tax Department now additionally includes the following shareholders: Lance A. Gildner (B.A., Indiana University, J.D., University of Dayton), Francis A. Kovacs, Jr. (B.A. & J.D., Capital University), and R. Brent Gambill, (B.A., DePauw University, J.D., Indiana University). R. Scott Blackburn continues to serve as the shareholder in the Estate Planning Department.

These departments naturally reflect the traditional practice areas of business law firms. Litigation, of course, has always had a major presence, as have its shareholder members: Robert P. Bartlett, Jr., Terence L. Fague (A.B., Wilmington College, J.D., Ohio State University), Janice M. Paulus (B.A. Ohio State University, J.D., University of Dayton), and Richard A. Talda (B.A., Wittenberg University, J.D., University of Toledo).

In the current economic and legal climate, the Firm has identified and created the Bankruptcy & Creditors Rights Department with Ron Pretekin as its shareholder member and the Environmental Department with Tim Hoffman as its shareholder member.

The successful development of these departments over the past twenty-five years is due in no small part to the significant contributions from both the shareholders and the associates within those respective groups, including a number

R. Scott Blackburn

Lance A. Gildner

Francis A. Kovacs, Jr.

R. Brent Gambill

Richard A. Talda

Jeffrey A. Mullins

Nicholas E. Davis, Jr.

Janice M. Paulus

who have moved on to other pursuits. The Corporate Department had the benefit for many years of the contributions of Doug Ventura (B.A., University of Notre Dame, J.D., University of San Diego) who gave up his shareholder status to join the Reynolds + Reynolds Company where he now serves as Vice President, Alliances and Acquisitions, General Counsel and Secretary.

Martiné R. Dunn (B.A., Northwestern University, J.D., University of Michigan) was a shareholder in the Real Estate and Corporate departments for a number of years before he returned to his home city of Cincinnati to develop his practice there. Marty Dunn had the distinction of becoming the first African-American shareholder in the Firm when he was admitted in 1992.

Leaving the Firm to go to the bench was Thomas M. Hanna (B.A. & J.D., University of Dayton, M.B.A., Capital University) who in 1990 was elected as Municipal Court Judge in the City of Kettering.

For 150 years, the Firm has reflected changes in the nature of the Dayton economy, the legal profession, and the level of governmental regulation. Looking back over its history, John Lombard identified 1964 as a watershed year. Within the Firm, Brad Coolidge's health was declining. Within the country Title VII was enacted and would soon be followed by many other regulatory laws, including the laws authorizing the EEOC, OSHA, EPA, ERISA, and a host of other regulations and cases creating or defining individual rights. As John Lombard observed, "This national shift from property rights to personal rights may well explain why highly qualified attorneys such as Brad Coolidge could individually serve as general counsel and why law firms now must have a cross section of highly specialized attorneys to effectively address the issues that confront businesses in today's environment."

The park bench wags may even suggest that the effort to construct and maintain a top notch law firm is now similar to constructing and maintaining a professional sports team. In an era when lawyers sometimes look like free agents, the key to success may depend on the ability to assemble, through associate development and mid-career acquisition, a combination that has the ability to work together and develop successful relationships with the business community of Dayton, the Miami Valley, southwestern Ohio, and beyond.

The Firm believes that its principals and developing associates are the key path to the future. At the same time, the Firm recognizes that those who came before us established the principles and character of the Firm, as well as much of the clientele. We recognize the contributions of those who have preceded us, not only the individuals discussed in this book, but also the Souls Who Once Were, lawyers who came and departed over the years, making their own marks in other venues.

As the Firm continues its efforts to provide a team of well-qualified lawyers who can meet the needs and expectations of its clientele, it accepts the corollary that these goals require patience and determination, building on the past and looking to the next 150 years of Cool Law.

EPILOGUE

Looking back at the Firm's first fifty years in a March 3, 1900, speech, Lewis Gunckel emphasized that the keys to great lawyers were *character, study,* and *work:*

> [H]igh character, close study – hard work. They became great by thorough education, profound knowledge of the law, undivided application, untiring industry, strick integrity, high sense of honor, entire truthfulness, religious fidelity to client, steady habits and pure life.

These goals are still espoused by the Firm, and we emphasize the principles of *character, study,* and *work* in our Mission Statement, while reciting them in a slightly different way for the modern market place:

> Coolidge, Wall, Womsley & Lombard will continue its history as the pre-eminent law firm in the markets it serves by:
>
> 1. Vigorously and professionally contributing to our clients' success.
>
> 2. Understanding the business of our clients and providing the expertise they need on a pragmatic basis to solve and avoid obstacles to their success; and

3. Earning the trust of our clients, our employees and the legal profession.

As we go forward to practice our legal and ethical principles in the future, we can learn from the principles of character, study, and work espoused in our past.

Merle F. Wilberding

APPENDIX 1

FIRM NAMES & FIRM ADDRESSES

1853	Gunckel & Strong	S.E. corner 3rd and Main
1854	Gunckel & Strong	S.E. corner 3rd and Main
1855	Gunckel & Strong	S.E. corner 3rd and Main
1856	Gunckel & Strong	S.E. corner 3rd and Main
1857	Gunckel & Strong	S.E. corner 3rd and Main
1858	Gunckel & Strong	S.E. corner 3rd and Main
1859	Gunckel & Strong	S.E. corner 3rd and Main
1860	Gunckel & Strong	S.E. corner 3rd and Main
1861	Gunckel & Strong	S.E. corner 3rd and Main
1862	Gunckel & Strong	S.E. corner 3rd and Main
1863	Gunckel & Strong	S.E. corner 3rd and Main
1864	Gunckel & Rowe	S.E. corner 3rd and Main
1865	Gunckel & Rowe	S.E. corner 3rd and Main
1866	Gunckel & Rowe	S.E. corner 3rd and Main
1867	Gunckel & Rowe	S.E. corner 3rd and Main
1868	Gunckel & Rowe	S.E. corner 3rd and Main
1869	Gunckel & Rowe	S.E. corner 3rd and Main
1870	Gunckel & Rowe	S.E. corner 3rd and Main
1871	Gunckel & Rowe	S.E. corner 3rd and Main
1872	Gunckel & Rowe	S.E. corner 3rd and Main
1873	Gunckel, Rowe & Gunckel	S.E. corner 3rd and Main
1874	Gunckel, Rowe & Gunckel	S.E. corner 3rd and Main
1875	Gunckel, Rowe & Gunckel	S.E. corner 3rd and Main
1876	Gunckel, Rowe & Gunckel	S.E. corner 3rd and Main
1877	Gunckel & Rowe	S.E. corner 3rd and Main
1878	Gunckel & Rowe	S.E. corner 3rd and Main
1879	Gunckel & Rowe	S.E. corner 3rd and Main
1880	Gunckel & Rowe	6 N. Main Street
1881	Gunckel & Rowe	6 N. Main Street
1882	Gunckel & Rowe	6 N. Main Street
1883	Gunckel & Rowe	6 N. Main Street
1884	Gunckel & Rowe	6 N. Main Street
1885	Gunckel & Rowe	6 N. Main Street
1886	Gunckel & Rowe	6 N. Main Street

1887	Gunckel & Rowe	6 N. Main Street
1888	Gunckel & Rowe	6 N. Main Street
1889	Gunckel & Rowe	6 N. Main Street
1890	Gunckel & Rowe	6 N. Main Street
1891	Gunckel & Rowe	6 N. Main Street
1892	Gunckel & Rowe	6 N. Main Street
1893	Gunckel & Rowe	6 N. Main Street
1894	Gunckel & Rowe	6 N. Main Street
1895	Gunckel, Rowe & Shuey	6 N. Main Street
1896	Gunckel, Rowe & Shuey	6 N. Main Street
1897	Gunckel, Rowe & Shuey	6 N. Main Street
1898	Gunckel, Rowe & Shuey	6 N. Main Street
1899	Gunckel, Rowe & Shuey	6 N. Main Street
1900	Gunckel, Rowe & Shuey	6 N. Main Street
1901	Rowe & Shuey	6 N. Main Street
1902	Rowe & Shuey	6 N. Main Street
1903	Rowe & Shuey	6 N. Main Street
1904	Rowe & Shuey	6 N. Main Street
1905	Rowe & Shuey	511 U.B. Building[1]
1906	Rowe & Shuey	511 U.B. Building
1907	Rowe, Shuey, Matthews & James	511 U.B. Building
1908	Rowe, Shuey, Matthews & James	511 U.B. Building
1909	Rowe, Shuey, Matthews & James	511 U.B. Building
1910	Rowe, Shuey, Matthews & James	511 U.B. Building
1911	Matthews, James & Matthews	511 U.B. Building
1912	Matthews, James & Matthews	511 U.B. Building
1913	Lee Warren James	511 U.B. Building
1914	Lee Warren James	511 U.B. Building
1915	Lee Warren James	511 U.B. Building
1916	James & Coolidge	511 U.B. Building
1917	James & Coolidge	511 U.B. Building
1918	James & Coolidge	511 U.B. Building
1919	James & Coolidge	511 U.B. Building
1920	James & Coolidge	N.E. corner 2nd & Main, #304[2]
1921	James & Coolidge	N.E. corner 2nd & Main, #304
1922	James & Coolidge	N.E. corner 2nd & Main, #304
1923	James & Coolidge	N.E. corner 2nd & Main, #304
1924	James & Coolidge	N.E. corner 2nd & Main, #304
1925	James & Coolidge	N.E. corner 2nd & Main, #304
1926	James & Coolidge	N.E. corner 2nd & Main, #304
1927	James & Coolidge	N.E. corner 2nd & Main, #304
1928	James & Coolidge	N.E. corner 2nd & Main, #304
1929	James & Coolidge	N.E. corner 2nd & Main, #304
1930	James & Coolidge	N.E. corner 2nd & Main, #304

1931	James & Coolidge	N.E. corner 2nd & Main, #304
1932	James & Coolidge	N.E. corner 2nd & Main, #304
1933	James & Coolidge	N.E. corner 2nd & Main, #304
1934	James & Coolidge	N.E. corner 2nd & Main, #304
1935	James & Coolidge	N.E. corner 2nd & Main, #304
1936	James & Coolidge	N.E. corner 2nd & Main, #304
1937	James & Coolidge	N.E. corner 2nd & Main, #304
1938	Coolidge & Becker	1200 Callahan Building[3]
1939	Coolidge & Becker	1200 Callahan Building
1940	Coolidge & Becker	1200 Callahan Building
1941	Coolidge & Becker	1200 Callahan Building
1942	Coolidge & Becker	1200 Callahan Building
1943	Coolidge, Becker & Wall	1200 Callahan Building
1944	Coolidge, Becker & Wall	1200 Callahan Building
1945	Coolidge, Becker & Wall	1200 Callahan Building
1946	Coolidge, Becker & Wall	1200 Callahan Building
1947	Coolidge, Becker & Wall	1200 Callahan Building
1948	Coolidge, Becker & Wall	1200 Callahan Building
1949	Coolidge, Becker & Wall	1200 Callahan Building
1950	Coolidge. Becker & Wall	1200 Callahan Building
1951	Coolidge, Becker, Wall & Wood	1200 Callahan Building
1952	Coolidge, Becker, Wall & Wood	1200 Callahan Building
1953	Coolidge, Becker, Wall & Wood	1200 Callahan Building
1954	Coolidge, Becker, Wall & Wood	1200 Callahan Building
1955	Coolidge, Wall & Wood	1200 Callahan Building
1956	Coolidge, Wall & Wood	1200 Callahan Building
1957	Coolidge, Wall & Wood	12th floor, Gem Savings Building4
1958	Coolidge, Wall & Wood	12th floor, Gem Savings Building
1959	Coolidge, Wall & Wood	12th floor, Gem Savings Building
1960	Coolidge, Wall & Wood	12th floor, Gem Savings Building
1961	Coolidge, Wall & Wood	12th floor, Gem Savings Building
1962	Coolidge, Wall & Wood	12th floor, Gem Savings Building
1963	Coolidge, Wall & Wood	12th floor, Gem Savings Building
1964	Coolidge, Wall & Wood	12th floor, Gem Savings Building
1965	Coolidge, Wall & Wood	12th floor, Gem Savings Building
1966	Coolidge, Wall & Wood	12th floor, Gem Savings Building
1967	Coolidge, Wall & Wood	12th floor, Gem Savings Building
1968	Coolidge, Wall, Wood & Matusoff	33 W. 1st Street
1969	Coolidge, Wall, Wood & Matusoff	33 W. 1st Street
1970	Coolidge, Wall, Wood & Matusoff	33 W. 1st Street
1971	Coolidge, Wall, Wood & Matusoff	33 W. 1st Street
1972	Coolidge, Wall, Matusoff, Womsley & Lombard	33 W. 1st Street
1973	Coolidge, Wall, Matusoff, Womsley & Lombard	33 W. 1st Street

1974	Coolidge, Wall, Matusoff, Womsley & Lombard	33 W. 1st Street
1975	Coolidge, Wall, Matusoff, Womsley & Lombard	33 W. 1st Street
1976	Coolidge, Wall, Matusoff, Womsley & Lombard	33 W. 1st Street
1977	Coolidge, Wall, Matusoff, Womsley & Lombard	33 W. 1st Street
1978	Coolidge, Wall, Matusoff, Womsley & Lombard	33 W. 1st Street
1979	Coolidge, Wall, Matusoff, Womsley & Lombard	33 W. 1st Street
1980	Coolidge, Wall, Matusoff, Womsley & Lombard	33 W. 1st Street
1981	Coolidge, Wall, Matusoff, Womsley & Lombard	33 W. 1st Street
1982	Coolidge, Wall, Matusoff, Womsley & Lombard	33 W. 1st Street
1983	Coolidge, Wall, Womsley & Lombard	33 W. 1st Street
1984	Coolidge, Wall, Womsley & Lombard	33 W. 1st Street
1985	Coolidge, Wall, Womsley & Lombard	33 W. 1st Street
1986	Coolidge, Wall, Womsley & Lombard	33 W. 1st Street
1987	Coolidge, Wall, Womsley & Lombard	33 W. 1st Street
1988	Coolidge, Wall, Womsley & Lombard	33 W. 1st Street
1989	Coolidge, Wall, Womsley & Lombard	33 W. 1st Street
1990	Coolidge, Wall, Womsley & Lombard	33 W. 1st Street
1991	Coolidge, Wall, Womsley & Lombard	33 W. 1st Street
1992	Coolidge, Wall, Womsley & Lombard	33 W. 1st Street
1993	Coolidge, Wall, Womsley & Lombard	33 W. 1st Street
1994	Coolidge, Wall, Womsley & Lombard	33 W. 1st Street
1995	Coolidge, Wall, Womsley & Lombard	33 W. 1st Street
1996	Coolidge, Wall, Womsley & Lombard	33 W. 1st Street
1997	Coolidge, Wall, Womsley & Lombard	33 W. 1st Street
1998	Coolidge, Wall, Womsley & Lombard	33 W. 1st Street
1999	Coolidge, Wall, Womsley & Lombard	33 W. 1st Street
2000	Coolidge, Wall, Womsley & Lombard	33 W. 1st Street
2001	Coolidge, Wall, Womsley & Lombard	33 W. 1st Street
2002	Coolidge, Wall, Womsley & Lombard	33 W. 1st Street
2003	Coolidge, Wall, Womsley & Lombard	33 W. 1st Street

(Footnotes)

1 The United Brethren Building was located at the northeast quadrant of Fourth and Main Streets and is now known as the Centre City Building.

2 This was also known as the L. T. Cooper Building.

3 The Callahan Building was located at the northeast quadrant of Third and Main Street.

4 In 1957, the Callahan Building changed hands and thereafter became known as the Gem Savings Building.

APPENDIX 2

LETTER FROM LEWIS GUNCKEL TO HIRAM STRONG, JULY 8, 1863

Dayton, July 8th, 1863

Col. Hiram Strong

I have been intending to write you for some time past, but ever since my return, I have been so busy that I could not well do so. Our courts are all over now, and as there is little new business Coming in, I shall for several months to come have all the leisure I want. I have succeeded in closing up a good deal of our old business and in getting fees therefrom. You know of the result of the Thomas vs. White case, but I will have some things to tell you about it when we meet. He paid the judgment without levy, issued the execution, and drew the money. He <u>did</u> come in and ask about our fee, but when we commenced to talk about it, I found he had a small conception of <u>our</u> position and labours in the case. <u>He thought our labors about equal up</u>

to the last trial, although he knew you had commenced and prepared the brief. I insisted on $500 for our fee; he thought it too much, but wanted $700 himself. I told him "as he had the money he could retain what he pleased." So he paid us $500 which he finally did. Becky [Rebecca Thomas] afterwards paid $100 for . . . .

Besides these fees, I got $100 from Wilson Garlick . . . and the bill owing us from Twin Creek R.R. Co.

In settling up claim of Dayton Maltack v. John L. Covey, I found You had collected $106.50 which you had not paid over. I fixed this By charging you with that much money from fees and then paying it.

I find you did not charge yourself with the fees collected while at home. I found $172.89 from Housatonic Bank, $165.50 from Dibbler . . . What did you get from Horton. He paid, didn't he?

If you want any money for your family or for any other purpose, I can furnish it. Let me know if you have any need.

I shall have no trouble doing all the business during the summer, but little as much as anybody else.

Things never since the Rebellion broke out looked so brightly as now. The news is good from every quarter, but splendid from Grant & Meade. It begins to look as if we might now calculate on a speedy end of the War.

All accounts from you and your Regiment are of the most flattering Character. I see the

Hamilton & Eaton papers both praise you highly. So do all who come up from the Army. I am heartily glad to hear you are at last appreciated and fully too.

Write me & oblige.
Your old Friend,

Lewis B. Gunckel

APPENDIX 3

LETTER FROM HIRAM STRONG TO LEWIS GUNCKEL, JULY 17, 1863

HQ 93rd Ohio, Camp Reed
Tullahoma, Tennessee
July 17, 1863

Lew,

Your letter of the 8th was handed me today by Lieut. Brown. I must own that with the best intentions I have proved the most negligent of correspondents. I write regularly to my wife. I intend to write often to my father, to you and to Wil Conover, but the fact is my life here unfits me totally for anything outside of my regular routine of military duties. I have an ordnance account for the quarter ending June 30th to make out and forward to Washington. It is of great importance to me, and is a labor similar to, and no greater than making out an administrators account with which I am familiar and yet I can scarcely bring myself to work on it. I have started half a dozen letters to you which now lie in my portfolio unfinished. But before I say *anything more and before I forget it I want to dispose of business.*

My family are in no need of money. You can make use of all you get and leave settlement until I return. I thought I had charged myself with all I got when at home. It may be however only in my cash book. The $106.50 acct. for Casey I don't remember anything about, but I presume you are right. The $172.89 Housatonic Bank is right. As to Dibbler Mark & Morse my memorandum book shows $135.55 instead of $165.50 as you have it. I think the margin to my check to Herbert [Weakley] will show what I paid him on that account. That deducted from $500 is what I retained. I got $30 of Mrs. Clark, $30 I think of Horton and $145.27 of John Dodds. But I think my cash and checkbook will show it all.

I don't know what information you have about us and therefore don't know where to commence in an account of ourselves. I see from the papers that Rosecrans has been very successful in concealing his movements from the public. After lying quietly at Murfreesboro for six months, we got an order in the evening of the 23d of June to march next morning at five o'clock with three days rations in haversack and nine days rations and ten days forage in the wagons. We had received similar orders frequently, but everyone guessed from some undefinable something about the order, and other appearances of preparation that this time we would go. And sure enough at the appropriate time we were off. The weather had for a long time been fine and the roads good. But that morning it began to rain and from that day, Wednesday, until Thursday July 2d at one o'clock in the morning, when we reached Tullahoma, we underwent more fatigue and suffered more from exposure and hardships that I have yet experienced in the army. It rained incessantly. We had little sleep and that in the mud and water. But nevertheless I never saw troops stand it as did all that came under my observation. In my own regiment the great difficulty was not to prevent the men from falling back and straggling to the rear, but to prevent them from getting ahead of me. I actually needed an advanced instead of a rear guard. And then too, under the severest trials the men were in good spirits – even joyous. We have some good singers and once about midnight when nearing Manchester they made the dark dismal woods sing with music while they were walking to the middle in mud and water and my regiment was not an exception. It was a fair sample of all. The fact is all of the regiments of our division are down to their fighting might. They have been freed from all of the sickly men and those who remain are able, and seem anxious for any duty that aids an advance towards the enemy.

The plan adopted by Genl. Rosecrans as we now see it, seems to have been singularly well adapted to the end in view and well executed. His object was to seize this place and Shelbyville. Either place cold be taken by an attach in front, and the difficulty in flanking them was caused by the fact that between them and Murfreesboro there was a high range of hills or mountains as they call them here – in fact a spur or offshoot from the Cumberland Mountains. The roads through this traverse contain passes which are easily defended by a small force, and that force would be very apt to ascertain, and give warning of any attempt to concentrate on any one road. Rosecrans determined to advance with the main body upon Manchester by way of Hoovers Gap. If he could succeed in concentrating his army at Manchester the enemy would be compelled to come out and fight him or fall back towards Chattanooga. For we see now, and he perhaps knew then that the works here were but slight defenses against an army advancing from Manchester. In execution of his plan he ordered our corps to advance upon the two roads leading directly towards Shelbyville while the center and left advanced slowly upon the Manchester roads. Our division advanced upon Liberty Gap which we attacked about noon on the first day and by night entered the Gap and took positions in it which we could easily maintain against a large force. It was defended by our brigade of rebels. We did not go through it but were ordered to hold it. Next day the rebels brought up two divisions and attacked Willich's brigade which was in advance but were repulsed. On the evening of the third day at 8 o'clock we left merely a picket line and made a forced night march for Hoovers Gap on the Manchester road. We got there with out whole corps at noon of the next day and found that Thomas had already taken the town of Beech Grove which was in the Gap and had advanced upon and got possession of Manchester. We rested until next day when we pushed on to Manchester, arriving there in the morning after another severe nights march. The enemy were then concentrating at Tullahoma and we expected a big fight. We left Manchester at noon with instructions to take before night the position we were to occupy in the next days battle. We had disencumbered ourselves of all extra baggage or rather of all baggage and until five o'clock in the afternoon marched at most rapid pace. By that time we received the news that the rebels had that morning evacuated this place. We then continued our march more leisurely and arrived here at 1 a.m. Thursday morning. I came into town with every man I started with but one and he came up in a few hours. Here we have been ever since. The rebels were most thoroughly puzzled in our movements. In the first place they had no idea we were advancing in force on Liberty Gap but after we had so easily driven them out of it they concluded that the main force was there. So they concentrated at Bell Buckel 3 miles from us to prevent our advance. When they discovered their mistake it was too late to prevent us from getting into Manchester which was not fortified at all, and once there we could take them in the rear. I find I have written more about this than I intended. But I was anxious to give you a correct idea of what was done, for it will give you confidence in and increase your admiration for General Rosecrans. I fear he will never get credit for what he has done simply because he fought no big battle, although he has shown more strategic skill than in the advance on Murfreesboro.

I might fill another sheet with what I have seen and heard in my own personal experiences. But I want to say a word as to the future prospects. As you say, things never looked brighter. They give us good hope that our troubles will soon be over. Having lost Mississippi I don't see how the rebels are going to maintain themselves much longer, whatever may be the issue of their Potomac campaign. The fact is they are entirely disheartened. We see rebel prisoners here every day. Deserters from Bragg's army are coming into our picket lines every day in crowds of tens and twenties. They all tell the same story as to the demoralized condition of their forces. A Virginian when questioned the other day as to whether he was tired fighting said he "did not mind the fighten" but this damned goen back was what he did not like." Then again the citizens of this place although professedly and openly disloyal say they want peace on any terms. They don't care which whips so that the war is ended. All that I have seen – Tennesseeans, Mississippians, Arkansians, Virginians – all unite in cursing South Carolina, and are prepared to rejoice when we take Charleston. I believe all of the people are thoroughly tired of the war, and whenever the hands of the leaders are stricken down, they will at once submit. All talk about retiring to mountain fortresses and fighting on every hill top is bosh. The people are prepared to go home and live in peace. I believe and hope we will be home in October. I may be mistaken, but that is my guess.

What think you of Brough's prospects? Is there any danger of disgracing the State by a failure to give him 50000 majority at least? By the way, how are we to vote here. Has provision been made for sending duly authenticated copies of the law to each regiment? This should be attended to as early as possible. Again, when the nominations are made committees should be appointed to inform the regiments of the names of the candidates and the offices for which they are nominated.

Nobody here regrets the Morgan Raid so far as we have heard from it. It will give the people at home a taste of war. Show them what they must expect if Ohio is made a border state. I wish Morgan had taken prisoner some of the men who should be, but are not in the army.

I was somewhat surprised at the division of the fee in the Thomas case. It looks to me like great illiberality. True neither of us was present at the last trial, but certainly what we did at the first trial should have entitled us at least to half the fee. Write me again when you can.

Yours truly,

Hiram Strong

PHOTO AND ILLUSTRATION CREDITS

Photograph by William Preston Mayfield of Callahan Building (1952). Reprinted with permission of Marvin Christian. All Rights Reserved.

Photograph of Winters Bank Building, courtesy of Bank One, N.A.

Photograph of Letter Press courtesy of William W. Streeter. All Rights Reserved.

Photograph of Firm Partners Behind the Gunckel Desk: ©1988 *Dayton Daily News*, All Rights Reserved. Reprinted with permission.

Photograph of Winters National Bank's Board of Directors in 1921, courtesy of Bank One, N.A.

Photograph by Merle F. Wilberding of Hiram Strong's Civil War sword courtesy of Isabel Frank Vandenberg, great grand-daughter of Hiram Strong.

Photograph by Merle F. Wilberding of 1850 "View of Dayton" lithograph used in end papers, courtesy of Isabel Frank Vandenberg and Dayton & Montgomery County Public Library.

Photograph of J. Bradford Coolidge's oil portrait, courtesy of Peirce Woodward and Schryver Photography.

Photograph of "The Spirit of St. Louis" train at West Casey, Indiana, courtesy of the Railroad Museum of Pennsylvania and Pennsylvania Historical & Museum Commission.

Photograph of "The Spirit of St. Louis" train car departing Union Station in St. Louis, Missouri, courtesy of the Rail Photo Service Collection of Joe Welsh.

Photograph of Hugh E. Wall, Jr., courtesy of the Hugh E. Wall, Jr., family.

Photograph of Merle F. Wilberding, courtesy of Schryver Photography.

Caricature of Lee Warren James, reprinted with permission of Curt Dalton. All Rights Reserved.

Photograph of Lee Warren James, courtesy of Dayton Country Club.

Reproductions of Martindale-Hubbell Listings of the Coolidge Firm, reprinted with permission of Martindale Hubbell.

Author's Note: I have made every effort to identify and trace the ownership of all photographs and other illustrations. If I have failed to give appropriate recognition and credit, I will do so in future printings.

LAWYERS AT THE FIRM

Robert B. Womsley
Ronald S. Pretekin
Jonas J. Gruenberg
Hugh E. Wall III
Glenn L. Bower
Fred A. Ungerman, Jr.
Richard A. Schwartz
Terence L. Fague
John C. Chambers
Barbara L. Sager
Jeffrey A. Mullins
David N. Reed
M. Shannon Martin
Nicholas E. Davis, Jr.
John C. Lombard
Roger J. Makley
Merle F. Wilberding
Robert P. Bartlett, Jr.
J. Stephen Herbert
R. Scott Blackburn
Sam Warwar
Timothy D. Hoffman
Janice M. Paulus
Francis A. Kovacs, Jr.
Richard A. Talda
R. Brent Gambill
Lance A. Gildner

Edie E. Crump
David P. Pierce
Jeffrey D. Snyder
Dina M. Cary
Christine K. Garcia
Christopher R. Conard
Timothy G. Pepper
Andrew D. Gleason
Douglas C. Anspach, Jr.
Steven M. Wachstein
Aniruddha D. Bhat
Matthew C. Gladwell
Robert S. Chelle
Kristin A. Finch
Lowell T. Woods, Jr.
Timothy M. Grimes
W. Kelly Lundrigan
Shannon L. Costello
Gregory M. Ewers
John T. Ernest
Jill A. May
Chad D. Hansen
Lisa K. Wiseman
Samuel E. Calabrese
Nicole M. Ruhenkamp

SELECTED BIBLIOGRAPHY

Allyn, Stanley C., *My Half Century with NCR* (1967).

Armour, Lawrence A., *The Young Millionaires* (1973).

Bambakidis, Elli, *Col. Hiram Strong: Special Papers Available in Dayton Collection* (Dayton & Montgomery County Public Library (2002).

Bank One, Dayton 175th Anniversary History (1814-1989).

Barney, E. E., *Education of Girls in Dayton – Cooper Seminary* (No Date).

Becker, Carl M., *The Village: A History of Germantown, Ohio* 1804-1976 (1981).

Beers, W.H., *History of Montgomery County, Ohio* (1882).

Bennett, Maxine, *The Gunckel Family* (1984).

Centerville Historical Society, *A Sense of Place* (1977 & 1985).

Centerville Historical Society, *"Once Upon a Town and Township..."* (1971).

Centerville – Washington Township Historical Society, *Normandy Farms: The Land and the Legacy of Richard H. Grant, Sr.* (2002).

Conover, Charlotte Reeve, *Dayton and Montgomery County: Resources and People* (1932).

Conover, Charlotte Reeve, *Dayton, Ohio: An Intimate History* (1932)(1995 Edition).

Conover, Charlotte Reeve, *Some Dayton Saints and Prophets* (1907).

Conover, Charlotte Reeve, *Story of Dayton* (1917).

Coolidge, J. Bradford, *Class Notes for Harvard Law School* (1910-1911) (8 Volumes).

Crew, Robert B., Interview (November 12, 2002).

Crouch, Tom, *The Bishop's Boys* (1989).

Dalton, Curt (Compiler), *Business Men of Dayton 1905-1906* (1995).

Dayton Daily News (Archive Materials).

Dayton & Montgomery County Public Library, "The Hiram Strong Collection – Family Papers of Colonel Strong, a Civil War Soldier, Lawyer and Leader in the Dayton Community."

Demoret, Alfred, *A Brief History of the Ninety-Third Regiment* (1898).

Drury, Reverend A.W., *History of The City of Dayton and Montgomery County, Ohio*, (1909) (Two Volumes).

Dube, Liz, "*The Copying Pencil: Composition, History and Conservation Implications,*" Book & Paper Group Annual (1998).

Dwight, Benjamin W., *The History of the Descendents of Elder John Strong of Northampton, Mass.* (1871).

Eckert, Allan W., *A Time of Terror: The Great Dayton Flood* (1997 Edition).

Edgar, John F., *Pioneer Life in Dayton and Vicinity*, 1796-1840 (1896).

Grant, Richard H., Jr., and Denlinger, Teri E., *Free Wheeling – 80 Years of Observations by the Patriarch of Reynolds & Reynolds* (1994).

Greer, David C., *Sluff of History's Boot Soles* (1996).

Gunckel & Strong, "Original Retained Copies of Correspondence of Gunckel & Strong – 1853-1863" (10 Volumes).

Gunckel, Lewis B., "The Bench and Bar of Dayton" (A paper read at a joint meeting of the Dayton Historical Society and the Montgomery Bar Association on March 3, 1900).

Gunckel, Patrick H., *Taxation of Costs in Federal Courts* (1904).

Gunckel, Thomas L., II (Editor), *Gunckel Family History* (1990).

Hagwood, Julia Shupert, *Gebhart / Gephart & Related Families 1609-1996* (1996).

Havighurst, Walter, *The Miami Years* 1809-1959 (1958).

Hentz, J.P., *Twin Valley: Its Settlement & Subsequent History*: 1798-1882 (1982).

History of the National Home for Disabled Volunteer Soldiers, written and compiled by a Veteran of the Home (Copyright 1875 by Chaplain Wm. Earnshaw).

Houk, George Washington, *A Sketch of the Dayton Bench and Bar* (1889).

Houk, George W., *Frank Hill Smith & The Dayton Hydraulic Co.* (2001).

Johnson, C. Terry, Interview (November 19, 2002).

Kern, Charme, *History of Germantown: 1804-1954* (1954).

L.M. Berry and the Yellow Pages (A History of the First 50 Years) (1960).

Lombard, John C., Interview (June 21, 2002).

Lowe, Charles D., Interview (October 23, 2002).

MacIntosh, Craig, and Frame, Robert, *Dayton Sketchbook* (1977 & 1985).

Marcosson, Isaac F., *Colonel Deeds* (1947).

Marcosson, Isaac F., *Wherever Men Trade – The Romance of the Cash Register* (1945).

Matusoff, Robert B., Interview (September 6, 2002).

McDermott, Clarke, *A History of the First Presbyterian Church of Dayton from 1845-1880* (1880).

Miller, Marcella, *A History of Germantown, Ohio & Biographical Sketches* (1962).

Montgomery County, Ohio – Cemetery Burial Records (Volume I, Books B-1 through B-4, Woodland Cemetery) (2001).

National Archives and Records Service: "Hiram Strong File."

NCR: *1923-1951: The Accounting Machine Era* (1984).

NCR: *A Chronology of the General Counsels of NCR – Over 100 Years of Leadership in NCR and the Dayton Community.*

Osteen, Mame, *History of Lakewood Cemetery* [Minneapolis, Minnesota] (1992).

Plavchan, Ronald Jan, *Inventory, Calendar, and Index of the Hiram Strong Papers 1862-1863* (1964).

Porzelt, Paul, *The Metropolitan Club of New York* (1982).

Proudfoot, W.B., *The Origin of Stencil Duplicating* (1972).

Pugh, Emerson W., *Building IBM: Shaping an Industry and its Technology* (1995).

Rhodes, Barbara and Streeter, William W., *Before Photocopying* (1999).

Ronald, Virginia, and Ronald, Bruce, *The Land Between the Miamis* (1996).

Shuey, D.B., *History of Shuey Family in America: 1732-1919* (2nd Ed.) (1919).

Steele, Robert W. and Steele, Mary Davies, *Early Dayton 1796-1896* (1896).

Strong, Albert, *The Strongs of Strongville* (1931).

Wall, Hugh E., Jr., Letter to Author (August 1, 1994).

Wall, Hugh E., Jr., Interview (May 31, 1988).

Wallace, Frank, *Knute Rockne* (1960).

Watson, Claudia, *Dayton Comes of Age* (2002).

Welsh, Joe, *Pennsy Streamliners – The Blue Ribbon Fleet* (1999).

Winters, Jonathan H., *A Sketch of the Winters Family* (1889).

Womsley, Robert B., Interview (May 10, 2002).

Young, Rosamond McPherson, *Boss Ket: A Life of Charles F. Kettering* (1961).

Young, Rosamond McPherson, "Newspaper History in City Colorful, Rich," *Dayton Daily News* (September 14, 1986).

Williams City Directories (Dayton, Various Years)

SELECTED LAW CASES

Bohn Aluminum & Brass Corp. v. Storm King Corp., 303 F.2d 425 (6th Cir. 1962).

Columbia Mill Co. v. Alcorn, 40 F. 676 (E.D. Pa. 1889), *aff'd*, 150 U.S. 460 (1893).

Dale v. Pattison, 234 U.S. 399 (1914).

Dayton Hydraulic Co. v. United States, 1976-2 U.S.T.C (CCH) ¶ 9788 (S.D. Ohio 1976), *aff'd*, 592 F.2d 937 (6th Cir. 1979), *cert. denied*, 444 U.S. 831 (1979).

Estoppey v. United States, 83 F. Supp. 840 (Ct. Claims 1949).

Grant v. Commisioner, 42-1 U.S.T.C. (CCH) ¶ 9446 (1942).

Hall v. Eaton, 139 Mass. 217, 29 N.E. 660 (Sup. Jud. Ct. Mass 1885).

Hauk v. Commissioner, 10 T.C.M. 925 (1951).

In re Appeal of Grant, 1 Ohio App.2d 84, 203 N.E.2d 859 (2nd App. District 1963).

Leidigh Carriage Co. v. Stengal, 95 F. 637 (6th Cir. 1899).

McEvilla v. Hall & Shelvin Lumber Co., 43 F. 139 (D. Minn. 1890).

McQuillen v. National Cash Register, 13 F. Supp 53 (D. Md. 1935) (First Opinion), 22 F. Supp. 867 (D. Md. 1938) (Second

Opinion), 27 F. Supp. 639 (D. Md. 1939) (Third Opinion), *aff'd,* 112 F. 2d 877 (4th Cir. 1940).

National Cash Register v. United States, 10 F. Supp. 687 (Ct. Claims 1935).

S.S. Kresge Company v. Dayton, 275 U.S. 505 (1927).

State of Ohio ex rel. Grant v. Kiefaber, 171 Ohio St. 326 (1960).

Torrent v. Duluth Lumber Co., 30 F. 830 (D. Minn. 1887).

United Iron Works v. Smith, 69 F. 827 (8th Cir. 1895).

USACafes v. Office, Case No. 8186 (Ct. Chancery Delaware 1985) (The case is unreported but posted on the internet at http://www.penweb.org/issues/energy/usacafes-dj.html (December 23, 2002)).

White v. Thomas, 12 Ohio St. 312 (1861).

Wickes v. Lockwood, 65 F. 610 (D. Minn. 1895).

SELECTED TOPICAL WEBSITES

Civil War Medicine: http://www.civilwarhome.com/civilwarmedicine.htm (August 17, 2002).

Dayton Old Soldiers Home: http://www.dayton.med.va.gov/museum.html (November 6, 2001).

Germantown History: http://www.mvcc.net/Germantown/gthistl.htm (January 21, 2002).

Gunckel Family: http://www.gunckel.com (November 6, 2002).

Morse Telegraphy: http://fohnix.metronet.com/~nmcewen/tel_off-page.html (May 14, 2002).

Cable Addresses: http://si.edu/lemelson/dig/westernunion.html (May 14, 2002).

Cable Addresses: http://westernunion.com (May 9, 2002)

Letter Copy Presses: http://officemuseum.com/copy_machines.htm (February 18, 2002).

Dayton Newspaper History: http://www.activedayton.com/ddn/info/history/cox.html (May 9, 2002).

Spirit of St. Louis Train: http://www.geocities.com/orvillei/prr41.html (September 23, 2002).

Nathaniel Strong House: http://www.mvcc.net/centerville/histsoc/nstrong.htm (November 6, 2002).

INDEX

COLOPHON

150 Years of Cool Law has been printed in New Century Schoolbook, an early twentieth-century version of the Clarendon font derived from Slab Serif (or "Egyptian") typeface. The paper is an acid-free eighty pound Finch Fine Vanilla text sheet manufactured by Finch, Pruyn & Company, Inc., Glens Falls, New York. The book has been printed at SpringDot, 2611 Colerain Avenue, Cincinnati, Ohio, and has been bound at Grummich Enterprises, Inc., 2838 Spring Grove Avenue, Cincinnati, Ohio.